D1609030

DATE DUE

5/27/09	

Multiprocessors

PRENTICE HALL SERIES IN COMPUTER ENGINEERING
EDWARD J. McCLUSKEY, SERIES EDITOR

ARMSTRONG   *Chip Level Modeling with VHDL*
McCLUSKEY   *Logic Design Principles*
RAO & FUJIWARA   *Error-Control Coding for Computer Systems*
TABAK   *Multiprocessors*
WAKERLY   *Digital Design Principles and Practices*

Multiprocessors

Daniel Tabak
Professor of Electrical and Computer Engineering
George Mason University

Prentice Hall
Englewood Cliffs, NJ 07632

Library of Congress Cataloging-in-Publication Data

Tabak, Daniel
  Multiprocessors/Daniel Tabak.
    p. cm.
  Includes bibliographical references.
  ISBN 0–13–605247–9:
  1. Multiprocessors. I. Title.
QA76.5.T29 1990
004′.35—dc20   89–16150
              CIP

Editorial/production supervision
  and interior design: Fred Dahl and Rose Kernan
Cover design: Wanda Lubelska Designs
Manufacturing buyer: Donna Douglass

© 1990 by Prentice-Hall, Inc.
A Division of Simon & Schuster
Englewood Cliffs, New Jersey 07632

Printed in the United States of America
10 9 8 7 6 5 4 3 2 1

ISBN 0-13-605247-9

Prentice-Hall International (UK) Limited, *London*
Prentice-Hall of Australia Pty. Limited, *Sydney*
Prentice-Hall Canada Inc., *Toronto*
Prentice-Hall Hispanoamericana, S.A., *Mexico*
Prentice-Hall of India Private Limited, *New Delhi*
Prentice-Hall of Japan, Inc., *Tokyo*
Simon & Schuster Asia Pte. Ltd., *Singapore*
Editora Prentice-Hall do Brasil Ltda., *Rio de Janeiro*

To the countries of my heritage and education

Poland, USSR, Israel, and USA

And to my Universities

Technion, Israel Institute of Technology, Haifa, Israel
University of Illinois, Urbana, Illinois, USA

List of Trademarks

Contents

Preface

In recent years, we have witnessed the widening spread in the development and implementation of multiprocessing computing systems. These systems are composed of multiple processors, interconnected to each other, and sharing the use of memory, input–output peripherals and other resources. Each of the processors is capable of executing a different part of the same program or a different program altogether. All in all, a higher system overall throughput is attained.

There are a number of multiprocessing research prototypes being developed in Universities and in industrial research laboratories. A significant number of companies offer commercial multiprocessors of different sizes and capabilities.

Multiprocessing is a particular case of parallel processing, involving concurrent execution of a number of computer operations. Computer arrays and pipelining are notable examples of parallel processing practices. Multiprocessors have been included so far in books dealing with parallel processing in general, featuring multiprocessors as a particular case. In view of the widening use of multiprocessors, it was felt that there is a need of a separate text, concentrating on this important aspect of parallel processing. It is the purpose of this book to fill this need.

The book introduces the reader into the basic principles of multiprocessors, covering their definition, structure, architecture, organization, design, and selected applications. Examples of some notable commercial multiprocessors and some research prototypes are presented. A basic knowledge of computer organization, covered by texts of Hayes or Hamacher et al., is assumed. The book can be used by advanced undergraduate (senior) or first-year graduate students majoring in Electrical and Computer Engineering or Computer Science, and by practicing engineers interested in multiprocessors. Although there are very few courses in Universities, dedicated exclusively to Multiprocessors, there are many Computer Architecture courses covering this topic in detail. This book could be used as a second text in such a course.

The book includes 15 chapters. Chapter 1 introduces the reader to the basic concept of multiprocessing, explaining the differences between it and other forms of parallel processing. Chapter 2 presents the basic structure of multiprocessors, stressing the importance of communication networks within the multiprocessor and discussing the problem of the communication overhead and its influence on the system performance. Chapter 3 is dedicated to the description of various software structures implemented in multiprocessors including semaphores, message passing, and an overview of concurrent languages. Multiprocessor operating systems, their basic properties and actual examples, are covered in Chapter 4. Chapter 5 presents some of the basic problems encountered in the design of multiprocessors, such as synchronization, memory latency, and cache coherency. An approximate method of evaluating the potential performance of multiprocessors, is presented in Chapter 6. Chapters 1 through 6 constitute the first part of the book, dealing with the basic concepts of multiprocessing.

Part Two of the book, consisting of Chapters 7 through 11, presents a number of selected examples of existing commercial multiprocessors. Any particular design features encountered in Part Two, which were discussed in general in Part One, are cross referenced to the appropriate chapter or section. The Alliant system was chosen to be presented in detail in Chapter 7 because of the versatility of its features and its widespread use all over the world. Chapter 8 covers bus-oriented systems such as the ELXSI, Sequent and Encore. The Cube systems are presented in Chapter 9, including the NCUBE, Intel iPSC and the FPS T-series. Chapter 10 discusses the switch network systems such as the BBN Butterfly and the crossbar IP-1. Chapter 11 features multiprocessing capabilities of advanced 32-bit microprocessors of Motorola, Intel, and National Semiconductors.

Part Three, including Chapters 12 through 15, constitutes an overall evaluation, comparison and some implementation examples of multiprocessors. Chapter 12 surveys the ways in which some design problems, discussed in Part One, are actually realized on existing research and commercial multiprocessors. In addition to the systems covered in Part Two, some notable research multiprocessors, such as the University of Illinois CEDAR, New York University Ultracomputer and IBM RP3 are discussed. A comparison of the basic data of the commercial systems, described in Part Two, along with some experimental benchmark results, are featured in Chapter 13. The selected multiprocessor implementation to be described in this book is real-time processing. This is done in Chapter 14. Concluding comments are given in Chapter 15.

The references are distributed among the chapters. Following Chapter 15 are the glossaries of abbreviations and terms for the convenience of the reader. Problems are concentrated at the end, to be assigned at the discretion of the instructor.

The author is indebted to many persons who have contributed to the preparation of this text. Valuable comments were given by Prof. Doron Tal of Florida International University, who reviewed the whole manuscript. Prof. David Kuck (University of Illinois) and Prof. Allan Gottlieb (NYU) have supplied detailed information on the CEDAR and the Ultracomputer, respectively. Useful comments on the commercial product examples featured in the text, were obtained from Phil Brownfield of Motorola, John Dutton of Alliant, Ron Cohen of Encore, Doran Wilde of NCUBE, Chris Drahos of Elxsi, Dr. Robin Chang of IP, and Jeffrey Baer of National Semiconductors. The manuscript was prepared by the GMU Word Processing Unit, under the direction of Ms. Mary Blackwell. The help of all of the above is highly appreciated.

The author would like to express his appreciation to Mr. James F. Fegen, my editor at Prentice-Hall, Inc. for his continued support and encouragement. Last, but not least, the author would like to thank his wife, Pnina Tabak, for her patience and understanding during the duration of this work.

PART ONE

BASIC CONCEPTS

CHAPTER 1

Introduction to Multiprocessors

From the very beginning of digital computer development, the designers always strove to increase the speed of operations. There are a number of possible ways to achieve this. An obvious approach is to improve the technology implemented in the realization of the computer components. The current technology has gone a long way in this direction and the development continues. There is of course a natural limitation in technology development; no signal can propagate faster than the speed of light. Another approach is to refine the logic design of computer subsystems to achieve higher speeds, for instance, use Carry Look Ahead, CLA in Addition, or the Booth Algorithm for multiplication [1]. Improving algorithms to solve various classes of problems will also lead to higher speed of operations.

There is, however, yet another way of increasing the speed of computation: by performing as many operations as possible simultaneously, concurrently, in parallel, instead of sequentially. This approach constitutes the basis of the following discussion.

In the traditional Von Neumann Architecture digital computer [1] operations were performed on a sequential basis. An instruction was fetched and decoded, the operands (if any) fetched, the operation executed, and the result stored, in that order. None of these operations was started until the preceding one was completed. A new instruction would be fetched only after the execution of the previous one was accomplished. There was no time-overlap in the execution of any of the elementary operations in the instruction cycle. Each *Central Processing Unit* (CPU) contained just one *Arithmetic Logic Unit* (ALU), which would perform all of the data processing tasks of the system.

As computers developed, more and more elementary operations were performed concurrently, on a time-overlap basis. For instance, the fetch procedure of a new instruction could be started before the previous one was completed. This was called a *prefetch* operation. In some systems an extra ALU was added. This development became particularly noted in the third generation of computer development [1, ch. 1]. For instance the IBM 360/91 and the CDC 6600 systems had a number of execution units, capable of operating in parallel, within the CPU [1–3].

The *pipeline* concept [1, 2] has also been implemented in practice in the third generation (on the IBM 360/91 for instance). The computer pipeline is analogous to the assembly line process in industrial manufacturing. A computer operation is subdivided into n stages, in each of which an elementary operation is performed on a set of operands. A set of operands would enter stage 1, where an elementary operation would be performed on it, the results of stage 1 are passed on to stage 2, where another elementary operation is performed, and so on, until the final results of the whole operation are obtained at the output of the last stage n. All n stages can operate simultaneously. Thus, an n-stage pipeline can be operating on a sequence of n sets of operands at the same time.

Both *arithmetic* and *instruction* pipelines have been developed. When the first set of operands enters the first stage of a pipeline, the rest of the n − 1 stages may be empty and idle. At the end, when the last set of operands leaves the nth stage, the preceding pipeline stages may be still unutilized. The pipeline is particularly efficient for long sequences of operands or in other words, for highly dimensional vector operands. For this reason, pipelined processors are also called *Vector Processors*.

As we can see, there is more than one way of performing concurrent operations on a digital computer. The possibilities are extended even more when the designers start adding more CPUs within the same system.

We can define the concept of *Parallel Processing* as a method of organization of operations in a computing system where more than one operation is performed concurrently (or simultaneously).

As we can see from the examples in the preceding paragraphs, Parallel Processing is a very general term; it can represent many different methods of its implementation. Just using the term ''Parallel Processing'' does not reveal what kind of a system we are dealing with and what exactly is performed simultaneously. We need to accept a detailed method of classification of parallel processing systems. Indeed, a number of classification approaches have been proposed in the past [1–3].

The most widely accepted and known method is the *Flynn classification* [4, 5]. To present Flynn's method, the following concepts will be used:

Pr   A processor, containing an ALU and additional logic.

CU   A control unit, controlling the Pr and other subsystems, by transmission of logic control signals, denoted here as instructions.

MM   Main memory, usually subdivided into a number of memory modules.

LM   Local memory, usually associated with a specific Pr.

I   Instruction (control signal) sequence (or stream).

D   Data sequence (or stream).

P   A complete processor, CPU, containing both an ALU and a CU.

If a number of any of the above exists in a certain system, appropriate indices will be added. For instance, for n processors, we will use the following notation: Pr1, Pr2, . . . , Prn. Flynn classification recognizes four basic types of systems (see Figure 1.1):

(a) *Single Instruction Single Data* (SISD) stream system (see Figure 1.1a). This is the basic single-processor, or *Uniprocessor* system. It may represent a classical Von Neumann architecture computer with practically no parallelism (IBM 701).

FIGURE 1.1a. SISD.

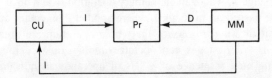

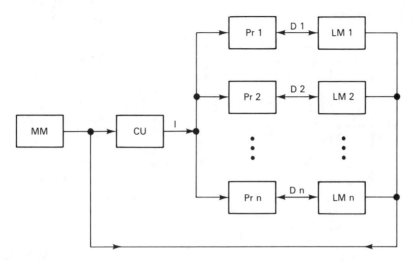

FIGURE 1.1b. SIMD.

However, it may also represent some more sophisticated systems, where certain methods of parallelism have been implemented, such as multiple functional units (IBM 360/91, CDC 6600, CYBER 205) or pipelining (VAX 8600), or both.

(b) *Single Instruction Multiple Data* (SIMD) stream system (see Figure 1.1b). A number of processors simultaneously execute the same instruction, transmitted by the CU in the instruction stream I. Each instruction is executed on a different set of data, transmitted to each Pri in a data stream Di from a Local Memory LMi, i = 1, 2, . . . , n. The results are stored temporarily in the LM. There exists a bidirectional bus interconnection between the MM and the LMs. The program is stored in the MM and transmitted to the CU. A system of this type is also called an *Array Processor*, because of the array of processors formed by the Pri, i = 1, 2, . . . , n. Examples of SIMD systems are ILLIAC IV, BSP, and MPP.

(c) *Multiple Instruction Single Data* (MISD) stream system (see Figure 1.1c). In this system, a sequence of data is transmitted to a sequence of processors, each of which is controlled by a separate CU and executes a different instruction sequence. The MISD structure has never been implemented. It resembles very much a pipeline structure. However, the main difference is that a pipeline structure belongs to the *same* CPU and is controlled by a single CU (see Figure 1.2).

(d) *Multiple Instruction Multiple Data* (MIMD) stream system (see Figure 1.1d). In the MIMD system we have a set of *n* processors *simultaneously* executing different instruction sequences on different data sets. This type of system is usually called a *multiprocessor*. Some examples are the IBM 3090, the Cray 2, the Alliant FX/8, and the NCUBE.

The MIMD systems (the multiprocessors) constitute the more general type of parallel processors. Any number of processors in the same computing systems execute

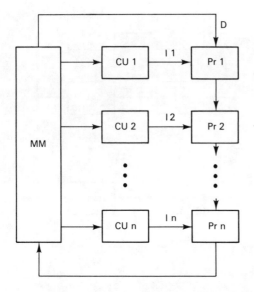

FIGURE 1.1c. MISD.

concurrently different programs using different sets of data. In general, no particular operation selection constraints are attached. Each processor can work on a different program at the same time. A program can be subdivided into *subprograms* (such as processes, tasks, and so on) that can be run concurrently on a number of processors. It is possible that in the same multiprocessor, some of the processors can execute parts of the same program, while other processors are busy running other programs. (See the example in Chapter 7.)

Multiprocessors are the topic of this text. Other types of parallel processors, such as SIMD array processors and pipeline vector processors, despite their widespread popular-

FIGURE 1.1d. MIMD.

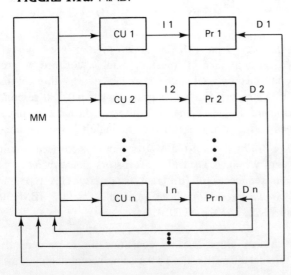

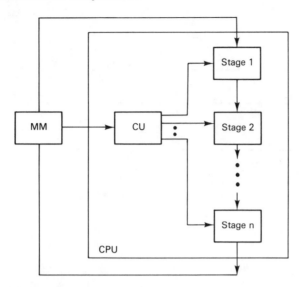

FIGURE 1.2. An n-stage pipeline.

ity, are outside the scope of this book. With the recent appearance of a significant number of commercial, relatively low cost, wide-spread multiprocessors, the topic of multiprocessors merits a separate text.

The Flynn classification is widely used in much of the professional literature. It is very general and may not reveal some important details on a number of systems. For instance, many processors (both uniprocessors and those within MIMD systems) have arithmetic or instruction pipelines, or both. The Flynn classification does not distinguish processors of this type. In fact, practically all computing systems manufactured since the mid-1980s implement pipelining. A different classification method, stressing the availability of pipelining and the number of pipeline stages, has been proposed by Handler [2, 6]. The *Handler classification scheme* features parameter values for:

(a) The number of processors, P.

(b) The number of ALUs under the control of a processor.

(c) Word length implemented in a processor.

(d) Number of pipeline stages in a processor.

(e) Number of ALUs that can be pipelined.

(f) Number of processors that can be pipelined.

Another classification method, proposed by Feng [2, 7], stresses the *degree of parallelism*, that is, the maximal number of bits that can be processed within a time unit by a computing system. For instance, the Carnegie Mellon C.mmp is a multiprocessor consisting of 16 processors of 16-bit wordlength. The *Feng classification* assigns to it the number pair (16, 16), since the system can process 16*16 bits simultaneously. The

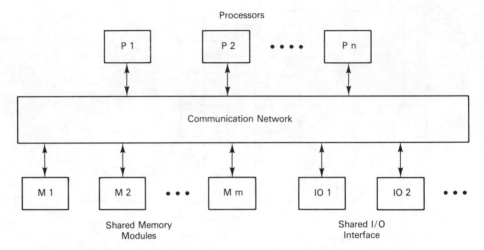

FIGURE 1.3. Tightly coupled multiprocessor.

Handler and Feng classifications, although of much interest, did not really "catch on," and are rarely used in the professional literature.

Despite Flynn's classification, the concept of multiprocessors is not clear cut and there is no concensus as to its precise definition. However, a widely accepted definition exists, originated by Enslow [8], pertaining to the characterization of a true, genuine multiprocessor. A multiprocessor, according to Enslow, must satisfy the following four properties:

(a) It must contain two or more processors of approximately comparable capabilities.

(b) All processors share access to a common memory. This does not preclude the existence of local memories for each or some of the processors.

(c) All processors share access to *I/O channels*, control units and devices. This does not preclude the existence of some local I/O interface and devices.

(d) The entire system is controlled by one *Operating System* (OS).

A multiprocessor, conforming to Enslow's definition, is sometimes denoted as a *Tightly Coupled Multiprocessor* [2] (see Figure 1.3). A *Loosely Coupled Multiprocessor* (see Figure 1.4) would tend to have much less shared and more local resources at the above points (b) and (c). Furthermore, a Loosely Coupled Multiprocessor is more likely to have additional OS environments at each individual processor. A Loosely Coupled Multiprocessor could sometimes be regarded as a *Computer Network*. So far, there is no standard terminology associated with the above concepts.

Loosely coupled multiprocessors are sometimes identified in the professional literature as *Distributed Systems*. Let us take a closer look at this concept. It so happens that a definition of Distributed Systems has also been proposed by Enslow [9]: A *Distributed Computing System* has

(a) A *multiplicity* of general purpose, physical and logical resources that can be assigned to specific tasks on a dynamic basis.

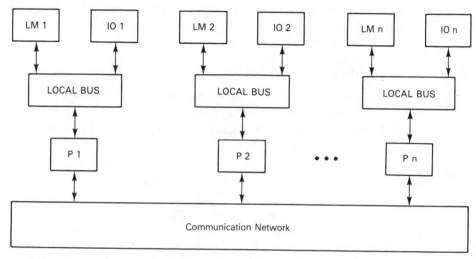

FIGURE 1.4. Loosely coupled multiprocessor.

(b) A *physical distribution* of the above resources interacting through a *communication network*.

(c) A high-level *Operating System* (OS) that unifies and integrates the control of the distributed components. Individual processors may have their own local OS.

(d) *System Transparency* which permits services to be requested by name only, without having to identify the serving resource.

(e) *Cooperative Autonomy* which characterizes the operation and interaction of both physical and logical resources. Although cooperation between resources is predesigned, the notion of autonomy permits a serving resource to refuse a request of service, or delay it, if it is busy processing another task. There is *no hierarchy of control* within the system.

   Comparing the definitions of multiprocessors and distributed systems, we can see that both have much in common. In fact, points (a) through (d) in the definition of distributed systems also hold true for multiprocessors. The main difference is in point (e) concerning the issue of *Autonomy*. A tightly coupled multiprocessor is usually centrally controlled. One of the processors is designated as a master and others as slaves, which have no autonomy. A loosely coupled multiprocessor would usually conform to the cooperative autonomy principle. Thus, it would be correct in most cases to accept the term of "loosely coupled multiprocessor" as synonymous to that of "distributed systems." However, since at this time there is no fixed standard terminology, the terms "multiprocessors" and "distributed systems" may continue to be used quite liberally in the professional literature. For the sake of being specific, Enslow's definitions will be accepted in this text.

When speaking about concurrency of operations in multiprocessors one should distinguish between the *levels* at which the concurrency is implemented. A *hierarchy of levels* has been defined in [10]:

1. *Job*, the highest level, consisting of one or more *tasks*.
2. *Task*, a unit of scheduling to be assigned to one or more *processors*. Consists of one or more *processes*.
3. *Process*, a collection of program *instructions*, executed on *one processor*. An *indivisible unit* with respect to processor allocation.
4. *Instruction*, a simple unit of execution at the lowest level (an instruction can also be decomposed into a number of microinstructions, though).

Different systems may implement concurrency on some or on all of the above levels. For instance, in a multiprocessor, each processor may run a separate job (program), or a separate task or a separate process (some authors assume the terms "task" and "process" as being identical; even by the above definition, a task may consist of a single process). Within a single processor, a number of instructions of microinstructions, may be executed simultaneously.

References 1. J. P. Hayes, *Computer Architecture and Organization*, 2nd. ed., McGraw-Hill, NY, 1988.

2. K. Hwang, F. A. Briggs, *Computer Architecture and Parallel Processing*, McGraw-Hill, NY, 1984.

3. J. L. Baer, *Computer System Architecture*, Computer Science Press, Rockville, MD, 1980.

4. M. J. Flynn, "Very High-speed Computing Systems," *Proc. IEEE*, Vol. 54, No. 12, pp. 1901–1909, Dec. 1966.

5. M. J. Flynn, "Some Computer Organizations and Their Effectiveness," *IEEE Trans. on Computers*, Vol. C-21, No. 9, pp. 948–960, Sept. 1972.

6. W. Handler, "The Impact of Classification Schemes on Computer Architecture," *Proc. 1977 Int. Conf. on Parallel Processing*, pp. 7–15.

7. T. Y. Feng, "Parallel Processors and Processing," *ACM Computing Surveys*, Vol. 9, No. 1, March 1977.

8. P. H. Enslow, "Multiprocessor Organization," *ACM Computing Surveys*, Vol. 9, No. 1, pp. 103–129, March 1977.

9. P. H. Enslow, "What is a 'Distributed' Data Processing System?," *IEEE Computer*, Vol. 11, No. 1, pp. 13–21, Jan. 1978.

10. D. D. Gajski, J. K. Peir, "Essential Issues in Multiprocessor Systems," *IEEE Computer*, Vol. 18, No. 6, pp. 9–27, June 1985.

CHAPTER 2

Multiprocessor Structure: Processing and Communication

A multiprocessor, whose basic structure was shown in Figure 1.3, is composed of *processors* (CPUs), *memory modules*, *I/O interface units*, and a *communication network* interconnecting all of them. The communication network is of utmost importance in a multiprocessor. The overall performance of the multiprocessing system depends not only on the individual speed and throughput of its processors; it strongly depends on the quality of its communication network [1]. This point will be discussed in detail later on.

From the standpoint of the type of the communication network, we can distinguish the following main categories of multiprocessor structures:

(a) Bus-oriented systems.

(b) Hypercube systems.

(c) Switch network systems.

A *bus-oriented system* contains one or more system buses (including data, address, and control lines) to which all of the system components are interconnected. A single-bus system is illustrated in Figure 2.1. A multiple-bus system is shown in Figure 2.2. (See page 12.)

A single-bus system is the simplest and least expensive to implement. It is used in a number of commercial multiprocessors, such as Sequent, Encore, and ELXSI (see Chapter 8). A single-bus system offers great configuration flexibility to both the user and the designer. Components and subsystems can be easily added to or disconnected from the bus. Unfortunately, this type of system suffers from some serious drawbacks. The most serious problem is the *bus bottleneck*. Only two devices at a time can establish communications through the system bus. Of course, a single device can transmit the same information to a number of receiving devices simultaneously, however, such an event is very rare. Usually, a processor Pi needs to access memory module Mj or an I/O interface unit IOk. It can be done one at a time, Pi, i = 1, . . . , n. Naturally, no matter how fast a bus is implemented, this bottleneck tends to slow down considerably the overall throughput of a multiprocessor.

If one of the individual components (processor, memory module, or I/O interface) fails, the multiprocessor can continue to operate, with a decreased computing power. All modern multiprocessors are designed for "graceful degradation" capabilities. However, a bus failure is a catastrophic failure in a single-bus multiprocessor.

These serious disadvantages of a single-bus system can certainly be alleviated if multiple buses are implemented [2]. Certainly, a failure of a single bus does not have

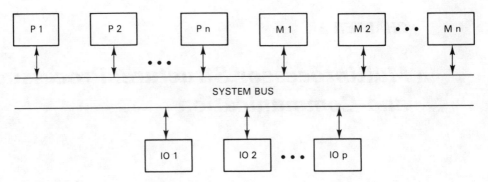

FIGURE 2.1. Single-bus system.

to be catastrophic for the whole system. If we have b buses, then up to b simultaneous interconnections can be achieved, alleviating the bottleneck problem. Of course, other problems arise. Looking at Figure 2.2, one can see that a multiport capability is implied for all subsystems. This is not a simple matter. *Multiporting* requires complicated and expensive extra logic on each device. Therefore, the number b can not be too high. A dual-bus system (b = 2) can be achieved at a reasonable cost. For instance, the Alliant has a dual system bus between its cache and main memory (see Chapter 7), and also a concurrency bus, connecting the processors (engaged in parallel data processing) only.

The *hypercube* multiprocessor structure is characterized by the presence of N = 2**n processors, interconnnected as an n-dimensional binary cube [3, 4]. Each processor forms a *node*, or *vertex*, of the cube. Each node has direct and separate communication paths to n other nodes (its neighbors); these paths correspond to the *edges* (channels) of the cube (see Figure 2.3). There are 2**n distinct n-bit binary addresses, or *labels* that may be assigned to the nodes. Each node's address differs from that of each of its n neighbor's in exactly one-bit position.

A *uniprocessor* (SISD), represented by a single node, can be regarded as a zero-

FIGURE 2.2. Multiple-bus system.

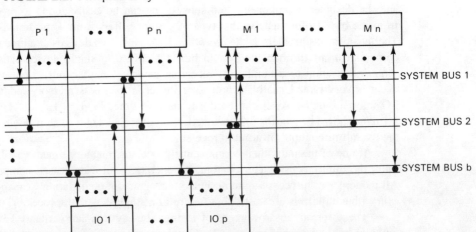

DIMENSIONS	NODES	CHANNELS	TOPOLOGY
0	1	0	
1	2	1	
2	4	4	
3	8	12	
4	16	32	
5	32	80	

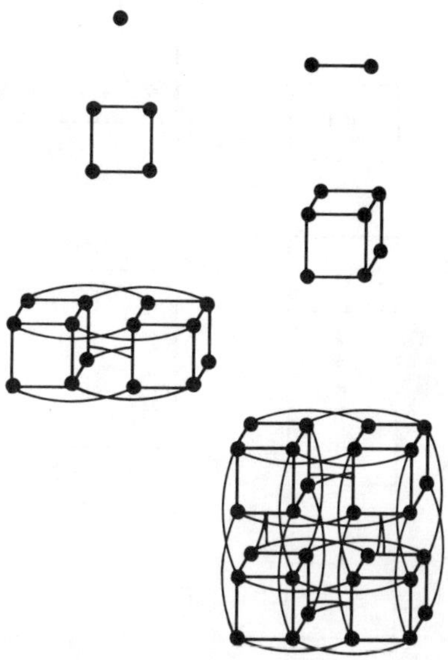

FIGURE 2.3. The hypercube topology (courtesy of Intel Corp.)

cube. Two nodes (processors), interconnected by a single path, form a one-cube. Four nodes, interconnected as a square, form a two-cube; eight nodes, interconnected as a cube form a three-cube, and so on (see Figure 2.3). The original Caltech cosmic cube [3], with 64 nodes, is a six-cube. The hypercube configuration is implemented commercially by NCUBE, Intel and Floating Point Systems (FPS). (See Chapter 9.) In all commercial hypercube systems the memory is distributed among the nodes; there is only local memory on each node board. In that respect, the hypercube multiprocessor does not conform to Enslow's definition; it is, indeed, rather a loosely-coupled system.

Since in a hypercube system each processor has its own local memory and it is directly connected to n other processors, the bottleneck problem seems to be less serious. Bear in mind however, that the interprocessor direct communication in the commercial hypercube systems, is *serial*, therefore limiting the overall bandwidth. The particular interconnection structure of a hypercube makes it suited for some classes of problems, but may prove to be very inefficient for others. The hypercube structure is certainly not considered universal.

The *switch network system* structure is much more general and offers numerous possibilities [5]. One of the most well-known switch structures is the *crossbar switch* (see Figure 2.4). The crossbar switch permits the establishing of a concurrent communication link between all processors and memory modules, provided the number of memory modules is sufficient ($n \leq m$) and that each processor attempts to access a different memory module. The same goes for I/O processors or I/O interface units (IOk). The information is routed through *Crosspoint Switches* (CS) (see Figure 2.5). A CS contains multiplexing and arbitration logic networks. If more than one processor attempts to access the same memory module, a priority queue can be established by the arbitration network. The main advantage of a crossbar network is its potential of high throughput

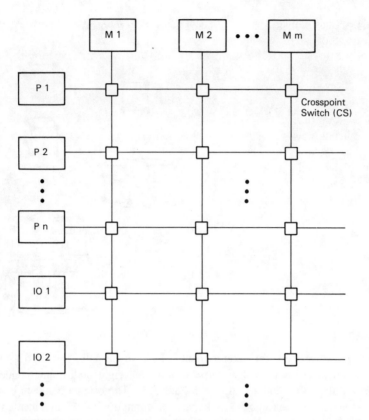

FIGURE 2.4. Crossbar switch multiprocessor.

by multiple, concurrent communication paths. Its main disadvantage is an exceedingly high cost and complex logic. Assuming n = m, we have n**2 CS units (disregarding the IOks). Thus the cost of a crossbar network with respect to n, is a quadratic function, n**2.

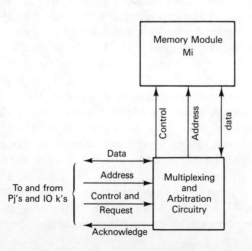

FIGURE 2.5. Structure of a crosspoint switch.

The crossbar network has been implemented in the Carnegie Mellon C-mmp [6]. The experimental C.mmp system was 16*16 (n = 16) and each processor was a DEC PDP-11 or LSIll. Commercial multiprocessors, implementing a crossbar switch, are the Alliant, between its processors and the cache modules (see Chapter 7), and the IP-1 with an 8*8 (n = 8) network (see Chapter 10).

A more general representation for multiprocessor switching networks is the *multistage network* or the *generalized cube network* [5]. It is shown in [5] that various types of multistage networks, introduced by other researchers (such as omega and banyan), are equivalent to, or particular to cases of the generalized cube network. For the sake of simplicity, the "multistage network" term will be used here. Descriptions of multistage networks can also be found in [1, 7–10].

A basic component of a multistage network is the two-input, two-output *Interchange Box* as shown in Figure 2.6. The two inputs and outputs are labeled "0" and "1." There are two control signals, associated with the Interchange Box, C0 and C1, which

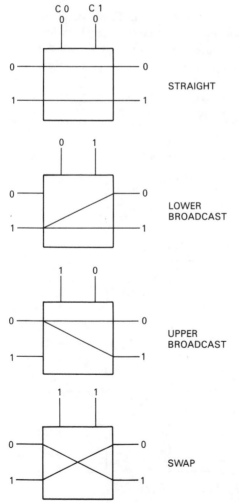

FIGURE 2.6. Interchange box states.

establish the interconnection between the input and the output terminals as shown in Figure 2.6 [5].

A general multistage network has N inputs and N outputs. In a generalized cube network $N = 2**m$, where m is the number of stages [5]. Each stage has N/2 interchange boxes. An example of such a network for $N = 8$, $m = 3$, is shown in Figure 2.7. The eight input and output links are labeled 0–7. Stage $i(i = 0,1,2)$ of this network contains the cube i interconnection function for each pair of input labels of each interchange box. If the binary representation of any link label is:

$$L = b_{m-1} \ldots b_1 b_0$$

then the cube interconnection function is defined:

$$\text{cube i } L = \text{cube } i(b_{m-1} \ldots b_1 b_0) = b_{m-1} \ldots b_{i+1} b_i' b_{i-1} \ldots b_1 b_0$$

for $i = 0,1, \ldots, m - 1$ and where b_i' is the logic complement of b_i. In other words, the cube i interconnection function associates link L to link cube i(L), where cube i(L) is the link whose label differs from L in just the i-th bit position. Thus in stage $i = 2$ the following links are paired:

0 000,	1 001,	2 010,	3 011
4 100,	5 101,	6 110,	7 111

FIGURE 2.7. Three-stage generalized cube network.

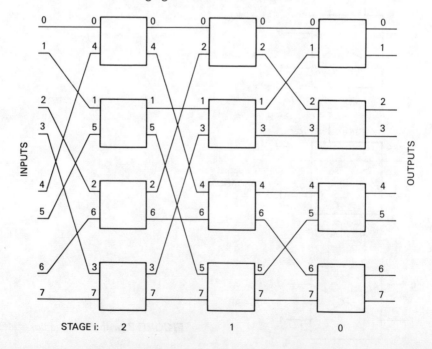

In stage $i = 1$:

0	000,	1	001,	4	100,	5	101
2	010,	3	011,	6	110,	7	111

and in stage $i = 0$:

0	000,	2	010,	4	100,	6	110
1	001,	3	011,	5	101,	7	111.

The cube i definition corresponds to the earlier definition of a hypercube, where the labels of two adjacent nodes differ in just one bit.

In a multiprocessor system the inputs and outputs of a multistage network can be connected to all of the processors (one input and one output to each processor), permitting direct intercommunication between them. Alternately, the inputs of the multistage network can be connected to the processors, and the outputs to the memory modules. When the number of processors N increases, the number of stages increases as $\log_2 N$, while the number of interchange boxes per stage is N/2. Thus, the total number of interchange boxes is $(N/2)\log_2 N$. (The number of crosspoint switches in an N-processor, N-memory modules crossbar switch is N**2.) Considering the fact that in actual systems, the communication through the interchange boxes is *serial*, we can see that the multistage system is a realistic and economic alternative to the crossbar. Of course, serial communication decreases the overall speed. This tradeoff of speed versus cost and circuit complexity will always have to be faced.

One of the basic requirements of performance from a multistage network is a combination of interchange boxes states which permit an interconnection between each processor and any other processor of the system. This capability is called *full access* [8]. When an interconnection between two processors is established, the state of the interchange boxes may be such that it is impossible to establish communication between some other pair of processors. A network where such an event can occur is called a *blocking* network. A network where there is a capability to establish an interconnection between any pair of processors, without blocking others, is called a *nonblocking* network. A crossbar is a nonblocking network, for instance. As a rule, nonblocking networks are more complicated and expensive.

One of the popular interconnections in multistage networks is the *shuffle connection* [1, 5, 7–10]. If we have N inputs, $i = 0,1, \ldots , N - 1$, the shuffle connection function is defined:

$$sh(i) = 2i + \lfloor 2i/N \rfloor \text{ (module N)}$$

An example of a single-stage shuffle connection (N = 8) network is shown in Figure 2.8. The $\lfloor x \rfloor$ symbol means rounding to the lower integer; for instance $\lfloor 1.5 \rfloor = 1.0$. Thus, for example

$$sh(6) = 12 + \lfloor 12/8 \rfloor = 12 + 1 = 13(\text{mod } 8) = 5$$

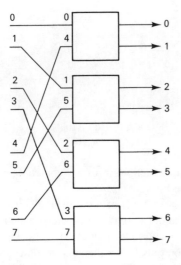

FIGURE 2.8. Single-stage shuffle connection network.

The shuffle connection is similar to shuffling a deck of cards, labeled 0,1, . . . , 7. By interweaving the first half, 0,1,2,3, with the second half, 4,5,6,7, the sequence 0,4,1,5,2,6,3,7 is obtained (see Figure 2.8).

A network constructed from m = $\log_2 N$ cascaded shuffle connection networks, is called an *omega* network. An omega network has been used in the New York University Ultracomputer [8,9]. It has been shown by Siegel [5] that the omega network is equivalent to the generalized cube network. (A three-stage example is shown in Figure 2.7.)

Another type of multistage network used in the industry is the *butterfly* network. Consider a binary label b_{m-1} . . . $b_1 b_0$. The *k*-th *butterfly function* Bk is defined for k = 1,2, . . . , m − 1 [8]:

$$Bk(b_{m-1} \ldots b_{k+1}b_k b_{k-1} \ldots b_1 b_0) = b_{m-1} \ldots b_{k+1}b_0 b_{k-1} \ldots b_1 b_k$$

Example: for m = 2, binary number $b_1 b_0$, k = 1

$$B1(b_1 b_0) = b_0 b_1$$

and specifically (Figure 2.9):   B1(00) = 00
B1(01) = 10
B1(10) = 01
B1(11) = 11

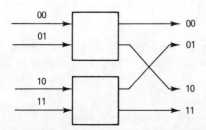

FIGURE 2.9. Single-stage butterfly network.

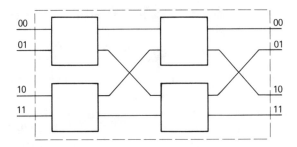

FIGURE 2.10. The butterfly switch.

By cascading two identical butterfly networks (see Figure 2.9), we obtain a 4*4 switch (see Figure 2.10). This is the basic switch unit which was first implemented in the Bolt, Beranek, and Newman, BBN Butterfly multiprocessor which will be discussed later in Chapter 10.

The properties of the various types of multiprocessor interconnection networks which we just discussed are summarized in Table 2.1. It is easy to see why the crossbar is rarely used due to its high cost and complexity as well as its difficult reconfigurability. The bus-oriented system, notwithstanding its bottleneck potential and lower reliability, is quite popular because of its low cost and ease of reconfigurability. Creation of low-cost, easily configurable multistage interconnection networks will most certainly cause their more popular use in actual computing systems. The BBN Butterfly is one of the pioneers in that direction.

The importance of the communication network in a multiprocessor can not be overemphasized. When a program is distributed among a number of processors for execution, there is always a need for transmission of intermediate results between the tasks which are scheduled to run on different processors. In fact, some processes will not be able to proceed without receiving the results from other processes. This calls for *synchronization* between different processes belonging to the same program. Even if all processors run different programs, the OS has to *schedule* and distribute the programs among the processors, keeping an eye out so that none of them remain idle. The communication network plays a crucial part in all of the above events since it has to efficiently transmit all of the data, intermediate results, scheduling, and synchronization control signals.

The need for scheduling, synchronization, and communication in a multiprocessor system, introduces an *overhead* in the system operation. Scheduling and synchronization

TABLE 2.1. Properties of various types of multiprocessor interconnection networks.

Property	Bus	Hypercube	Crossbar	Multistage
Speed	low	moderate	high	high
Cost	low	moderate	high	moderate
Reliability	low	high	high	high
Configurability	high	low	low	moderate
Complexity	low	moderate	high	moderate

depend, of course, on the algorithms used to implement them. However, their ultimate efficiency strongly depends on the quality of the communication system. Thus, it makes sense, to regard the overhead of a multiprocessor system as the communication overhead [1].

The throughput of a multiprocessor certainly depends on the number of processors and the quality of each individual processor configured into the system. However, an effort to improve the quality of the processors, without paying attention to the quality of the communication system, may prove counter-productive. If the communication overhead is too high, a single processor may handle a problem faster than a number of processors, working in parallel. Such a possibility can be illustrated by the following example [1].

Let us define R as a processing run-time quantum, and C as the length of the communication overhead produced by that quantum. The R/C ratio expresses how much communication overhead is incurred per unit of processing. Naturally, we should strive to decrease C while increasing the R/C ratio [1]. Let us assume a two-processor model, where the communication time is not overlapped with processing time (worst case). Now assume that we have M tasks, each task executing in R units of time and communicating with every other task on the other processor with an overhead cost of C units of time. No overhead C is incurred between tasks on the same processor. If we assign k tasks to one processor and M − k to the other, the total execution time is:

$$Et = R\max(M - k, k) + C(M - k)k$$

The first term, linear in k, represents the run-time, while the second, quadratic in k, represents the communication overhead.

Consider the linear, run-time term first.
For

$$M - k > k \quad \text{or} \quad M/2 > k \quad \text{we have:}$$
$$EtL = RM - Rk,$$

a straight line from $EtL = RM$ at $k = 0$ to $EtL = RM/2$ at $k = M/2$.
For

$$M - k < k \quad \text{or} \quad M/2 < k$$
$$EtL = Rk$$

a straight line from $EtL = RM/2$ at $k = M/2$ to $EtL = RM$ at $k = M$ (see Figure 2.11).

So far, just by looking at the linear term one can find a uniform, equal scheduling of tasks between the two processors; $k = M/2$, is recommended.

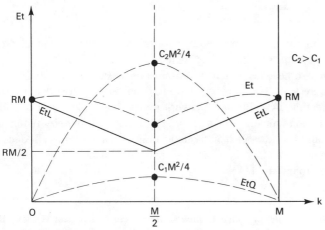

FIGURE 2.11. Two processor model execution time.

The quadratic term:

$$EtQ = CMk - Ck^2$$

crosses the k axis at $k = 0$ and $k = M$, and has a maximum of $CM^2/4$ at $k = M/2$.
The total Et at $k = M/2$:

$$Et(M/2) = RM/2 + CM^2/4$$

As long as $RM/2 + CM^2/4 < RM$, it is more efficient to schedule the tasks equally among the two processors. If the communication overhead C becomes too high, and we have

$$RM/2 + CM^2/4 > RM,$$

it will be more efficient and faster to schedule all of the M tasks on a single processor thereby taking up the shorter execution time $ET = RM$. In the above model we have to keep C at:

$$C < 2R/M$$

in order to have the two-processor system execute faster than a uniprocessor. It has been shown by Stone [1], that the above inequality is maintained even if the model is extended to N processors. Namely, for $C < 2R/M$ an even distribution of tasks between the N processors ($k = M/N$) is recommended, while for $C > 2R/M$, uniprocessor execution will be faster. The above inequality can also be rewritten as:

$$M/2 < R/C.$$

It shows that the higher the R/C ratio, the more tasks M can be run in parallel and faster than if run sequentially on a uniprocessor.

Conclusion

In addition to improving the processing capabilities of the individual processors in a multiprocessing system (by increasing their MIPS and MFLOPS figures), reducing the communication overhead as much as possible is basic to the design of an efficient communication system. The implementation of multistage networks is certainly a valid step in that direction. A multistage network (even if it is blocking) provides a number of parallel intercommunication links (contrary to the bus), thereby reducing the overall wait times required to establish communication. This, therefore, reduces the overall communication overhead C. A comparative analysis of some synchronous communication networks can be found in [11].

References 1. H. S. Stone, *High-performance Computer Architecture*, Addison-Wesley, Reading, MA, 1987 (Chapter 6).

2. T. N. Mudge, J. P. Hayes, D. C. Winsor, "Multiple Bus Architectures," *IEEE Computer*, Vol. 20, No. 6, pp. 42–48, June 1987.

3. C. L. Seitz, "The Cosmic Cube," *Comm. ACM*, Vol. 28, No. 1, pp. 22–23, Jan. 1985.

4. J. P. Hayes, T. Mudge, Q. F. Stout, S. Colley, J. Palmer, "A Microprocessor-based Hypercube Supercomputer," *IEEE MICRO*, Vol. 6, No. 5, pp. 6–17, Oct. 1986.

5. H. J. Siegel, *Interconnection Networks for Large-scale Parallel Processing*, Lexington Books, D. C. Heath and Co., Lexington, MA, 1985.

6. D. P. Siewiorek, et al., "A Case Study of C.mmp, Cm*, and C.vmp," *Proc. IEEE*, Vol. 66, No. 10, pp. 1178–1199, Oct. 1978.

7. K. Hwang, F. A. Briggs, *Computer Architecture and Parallel Processing*, McGraw-Hill, NY, 1984 (Chapter 7).

8. J. P. Hayes, *Computer Architecture and Organization*, *2nd. ed.*, McGraw-Hill, NY, 1988 (Chapter 7).

9. G. S. Almasi, A. Gottlieb, *Highly Parallel Computing*, Benjamin/Cummings, Redwood City, CA, 1989.

10. V. M. Milutinovic, ed., *Computer Architecture: Concepts and Systems*, North-Holland, Amsterdam, 1988.

11. L. N. Bhuyan, Q. Yang, D. P. Agrawal, "Performance of Multiprocessor Interconnection Networks," *IEEE Computer*, Vol. 22, No. 2, pp. 25–37, Feb. 1989.

CHAPTER 3

Multiprocessor Software

3.1 Parallelization

There is no sense in building an expensive multiprocessor if we can not utilize it efficiently; if we can not program it. Creating efficient multiprocessor software is one of the most active research and development endeavors [1–12]. The most obvious and sound approach would be to program a given problem directly for a parallel processing algorithm, if possible. This would require

(a) The availability of a parallel processing language.
(b) The possibility to execute the algorithm in parallel.

Although some parallel processing languages have been proposed [1], the area is still under development and strongly machine-dependent. Many problems are not executable in parallel. In this case, the best approach is to schedule a different program on each separate processor. A vast amount of algorithms and software exists, implemented so far, on uniprocessors. A considerable amount of time and resources have been invested in this software and it can not be abandoned without incurring considerable losses. For this reason, it makes sense for many users to *parallelize* existing programs whenever possible. A number of parallelizing compilers have been created. An example is the Alliant FX/FORTRAN (see Chapter 7 for more details).

We distinguish two basic types of parallelization approaches [12]:

1. *Explicit parallelization*—performed by the user *prior* to loading the program, by specifying concurrency and by using special language constructs as provided in the OS. Such a capability is usually provided by multiprocessor manufacturers which do not offer an automatically parallelizing compiler.

2. *Implicit (automatic) parallelization*—performed automatically by the compiler.

The following discussion will concentrate on the automatic parallelization by the compiler. One of the main factors in a program, and of crucial importance in parallelization, is *data dependency*. This is, does a given part of a program depend on data generated in another part? If there is a dependency, then the part yielding the needed data, should be executed first and not concurrently. On the other hand, two parts (processes) of a program which do not use data generated by each can run concurrently. The parallelizing compiler scans the program to detect any existing data dependencies and any serial behavior. The other parts of the program, which do not exhibit serial behavior and

23

have no data dependency, are good candidates for concurrent scheduling on different processors. A general procedure for detecting dependencies by a parallelizing compiler could be the following [2]:

(a) List the names of the variables *read* and *written* along the program, particularly in loop iterations.

(b) If a name appears on both the read and written list, it can be a potential Read/Write (R/W) or Write/Read (W/R) dependency.

(c) All variables that are written are potentially Write/Write (W/W) dependencies.

(d) Examine each case to determine if an actual dependency exists. For a W/W dependency to exist, one variable has to be written by two different loop iterations.

Example: Consider the following part of a loop, at iteration i,

$$A(i) = B(i) + D$$
$$A(i - 1) = B(i) + C$$

At the previous iteration i − 1 we had:

$$A(i - 1) = B(i - 1) + D$$
$$A(i - 2) = B(i - 1) + C$$

There is a W/W dependency for A(i − 1), being written into in both iterations. On the other hand, if the iteration index increased by two, the previous loop would be i − 2 and in it:

$$A(i - 2) = B(i - 2) + D$$
$$A(i - 3) = B(i - 2) + C$$

No W/W dependency exists and the loops can be scheduled concurrently on separate processors.

As a matter of fact, iterative loops are the best candidates for concurrent distribution on a number of processors. In the automatic parallelization of iterative loops we distinguish two basic cases [7]:

Doacross—used when there are dependencies between different iterations. The execution of the loop iterations is distributed over a number of processors in ascending order; first iteration to processor P1, second, to P2, and so on. Appropriate delays may be introduced, until the data, causing the dependencies, is transmitted from the other processor. This is implemented in the Alliant FX/FORTRAN compiler, for instance (see Chapter 7 for details).

Doall—used when there are no dependencies in a loop whose iterations can execute in any order. The iterations can be scheduled on any processor, in any order.

Data dependency (or the lack of it) between two processes in a program can be established using the concept of *commutativity* along the time axis [12]. Two processes are commutative if they can be executed in any order without changing the results. Naturally, in this case, they could be scheduled to run concurrently. Commutativity is however a necessary but not a sufficient condition for parallel execution. In some algorithms (such as in FFT, involving bit reversal [12]) there may be statements which can be executed in either order but not in parallel.

The *Bernstein Condition* [13] establishes more stringent rules for parallelizability of two processes. Consider a set of processes Ti (i = 1,2, . . .). Define for each process:

(a) The *Read Set*, Ri, representing the set of all memory locations for which the first operation in Ti involving them is a *fetch* (read memory).

(b) The *Write Set*, Wi, representing the set of all locations that are stored into (write memory) in Ti.

The conditions under which two sequential processes T1 and T2 can be executed as two independent concurrent processes are:

1. Locations in R1 must not be destroyed by storing operations in W2. In other words,

$$R1 \text{ AND } W2 = E \text{ (the empty set)}.$$

2. By symmetry, exchanging the roles of T1 and T2:

$$R2 \text{ AND } W1 = E.$$

3. If, after executing T1 and T2 in parallel, and another process, say T3, is entered, R3 must be independent of the storing operations in T1 and T2, that is:

$$(W1 \text{ AND } W2) \text{ AND } R3 = E.$$

The above points of the Bernstein Condition can be implemented in a parallelizing compiler.

3.2 Parallel Programming Structures

One of the most convenient programming structures for parallel execution scheduling are loop iterations. One can use the following do statements to distinguish between sequential and parallel execution scheduling [2]:

do seq—execute loop iterations sequentially.

do par—execute loop iterations in parallel.

Example: Suppose we have to perform an iteration denoted by ITR, I times. If we have only a single processor, we would have to perform I serial executions of ITR:

for i = 1 to I do seq

begin

ITR

end do seq.

If on the other hand, we have I processors available, the following structure:

for i = 1 to I do par

begin

ITR

end do par

causes I copies of ITR to be activated and executed concurrently, for different values of i, on the I processors. Assuming no dependencies, this would correspond to the *doall* case, as defined in section 3.1.

If there exist data dependencies between different steps of the iteration, a *barrier* can be introduced for synchronization of the iteration steps. No processor can cross the barrier until all processors performing the loop iteration have reached the barrier.

Example: Assume that the iteration ITR is composed of the following steps:

ITRa(i)

ITRb(i)

ITRc(i), i = 1, . . . , I.

ITRc depends on results of ITRa and ITRb of prior iterations. In this case a barrier is introduced between ITRb and ITRc; it forces all iterations of ITRa and ITRb to complete before any ITRc is started. The structure is as follows:

for i = 1 to I do par

begin

ITRa(i)

ITRb(i)

Barrier

ITRc(i)

end i loop.

This case would entail a larger communication overhead for transmitting intermediate results between the processors and introducing wait states due to the barrier. It corresponds to the *doacross* case, as defined in section 3.1. The overhead may be reduced by judicious scheduling of different iterations (for different values of i) to be executed on the appropriate processors.

An alternate loop parallelization statement is the *for all*, terminated by a matching *end for* [3]. For instance,

for all Pi, i = 1 to I do

ITR(i)

end for

would activate I processors P1, P2, . . . , PI to execute the loop iteration ITR(i), i = 1, . . . , I concurrently, ITR(1) on P1, . . . , ITR(I) on PI.

Many programs are inherently sequential and can not be parallelized. However, some programs may be parallelized for a part of the execution. Assume the following structure of program SEQPAR:

SEQPAR: seq1

par1

par2

seq2

Parts seq1 and seq2 must be executed sequentially, as shown in the above order. Parts par1 and par2 must be executed between seq1 and seq2, however they can be executed concurrently. In this case, we can use the *fork* and *join* statements [3]. When the execution of seq1 is finished, the *fork par2* statement will cause par2 to be executed on another processor, P2 (assuming one is available), concurrently with par1 whose execution is continued on the same processor that executed seq1 (say P1). At the end of par1 a statement *join par2* is inserted. If P1 reaches join par2 before P2 finishes executing par2, P1 enters a wait state, until par2 is completed and its results communicated to P1. Then, P1 continues with the execution of seq2:

P1   *P2*

seq1

fork par2 --------->

par1   par2

join par2 <---------

seq2

The fork and join statements are used on the UNIX OS [14] and in other systems.

If a program contains a number of parts par1, par2, . . . , parI, that can be executed concurrently on I processors, the following statement can be used [3]:

$$\text{cobegin par1}\|\text{par2}\| . \ \ . \ \ . \ \|\text{parI coend}$$

Processing continues beyond the coend only after all the parIs have completed execution.

Statements such as fork, cobegin belong to the category of *Asynchronous Parallel Programming* [1], where processes or tasks are specified and scheduled for concurrent execution on separate processors. This certainly corresponds to the case of the MIMD multiprocessors. *Synchronous Parallel Programming* involves a sequence of instructions applied concurrently to different sets of data. This corresponds to the SIMD-type systems, not dealt with in this text.

Suppose we have a considerable number of program sections which can be executed concurrently. Should we capitalize on this and schedule each such section on a separate processor, or should we use less processors, scheduling larger parts of a program on each?

This brings us to the *Grain Size* problem, namely, what is the best size of a program module to be scheduled to run concurrently on a separate processor [6]. In this case, the "best" or optimal grain size will be the one yielding the shortest possible execution time. If a grain is too large, parallelism is limited. Some processors may be idle, thereby reducing the utilization of the system. Small grains maximize parallelism but may increase the communication overhead due to the possible increased amount of data transmitted between a larger number of processors. The optimum scheduling and grain size determination is somewhere in between and is very much problem dependent. If using small grains causes too much communication overhead, a number of small grains can be combined by *Packing* them into a single processor. The packing should be done to the extent of attaining minimal communications delays. The resulting optimal grain size and scheduling would usually be different for different types of programs.

3.3 Critical Sections and Semaphores

Most of the main memory in a multiprocessor is shared between the processors, by definition. The shared memory contains sections of data which is both accessible and modifiable by a number of processors. Suppose processor Pi has accessed a shared section and is in the process of modifying it. If another processor Pj attempts to access and modify the same section, erroneous results in the computation may occur before Pi has completed its access. Therefore, controlled access and *mutual exclusion* with respect to such sections is required. Modifiable sections of programs, shared by a number of processors, and executed as an *atomic* (uninterruptible) operation, are called *critical sections* [1–3, 12]. On the other hand, *non-modifiable* program sections (such as fixed tabular information), that can be shared, are called *reentrant*.

A number of mechanisms for mutual exclusion of critical sections have been developed [1–3]. Basically, when a processor accesses a critical section, any other access should be excluded (prevented) until the processor completes its access. One of the most popular methods of mutual exclusion is through the use of *semaphores*. Sema-phores were originally proposed by Dijkstra [15]. Of particular interest is the *binary semaphore* (an integer binary variable of 0 or 1). Only two operations are permitted on a semaphore:

1. *P operation* causes the semaphore's value to be decreased by 1, provided it is not zero. The name comes from the Dutch "prolagen," a combination of "proberen" (to try) and "verlagen" (to reduce): Also from the word "passeren" (to pass).

2. *V operation* causes the semaphore value to be increased by 1, provided it is not 1 already. The name comes from the Dutch "verhogen" (to increase) or "vrygeven" (to release).

Both P and V are indivisible, uninterruptible operations. The P and V operations are also called *lock* and *unlock*, respectively. The mechanism of mutual exclusion, using binary semaphores, works as follows. Each critical section has a semaphore associated with it. The semaphore is a location in the shared memory. A semaphore has a value *zero* if a process is executing in the critical section, associated with it; in other words, it is *busy*. Otherwise, when the access to the critical section is *free*, the value of its semaphore is *one*.

A process enters the critical section only if its semaphore value is one. It immediately performs the P operation, reducing the semaphore value to zero, and thus excluding any other process from this section. When the execution in the critical section is completed, the process performs the V operation, raising the semaphore value from zero to one, thus allowing another process to enter this section.

An alternate way of implementing mutual exclusion is by the use of a *monitor*. A monitor is a software construct [1–3, 12] which collects critical sections into a single structure where only one process can have access to this structure at any time. The critical sections are procedures or functions of the monitor.

The monitor defines a shared data structure and all the operations that can be performed on it. The operations are defined by the procedures and functions of the monitor. The monitor also defines an initialization operation that is executed when its data structure is created. A process can access the shared data of a monitor by calling one of its procedures. If there is more than one process in a queue, a process can append itself to a single condition variable by executing a *wait* operation. Another process, executing a *signal* operation on a condition variable queue, will cause a process delayed in that queue to be resumed. A monitor may include the implementation of semaphores and it usually is a part of the Operating System (OS), to be discussed in Chapter 4.

Sometimes the concept of the *conditional critical section* is implemented [1, 12]. In that case, a process can enter and execute a critical section only if a predefined logical condition is satisfied (true), in addition to the critical section being free.

The capability of managing critical sections and semaphores is supported by a number of special machine language instructions. These instructions are supported by the basic hardware design in a number of existing computing systems.

A well-known representative of such instructions is the *Test And Set* (TAS) [2]. It is an indivisible, uninterruptible instruction, operating with a *Read/Modify/Write* (RMW) bus cycle. It tests whether a certain variable (Read), located in memory (a semaphore, for instance), is zero or not, and sets the condition code flags accordingly. It then proceeds to set the value of that variable to one (Modify/Write).

Another form of an indivisible instruction, used to update shared data, is the *Compare And Swap* (CAS). A shared data item is locked at the beginning of the execution of CAS, compared with the contents of a *compare register*, setting condition code flags accordingly, and then updated by moving into it the contents of an *update register*. After that, the access to the shared data item is unlocked, and the execution of CAS is complete. The implementation of instructions such as TAS or CAS in a given computing system, provides the system with synchronization capabilities for multiprocessing operation. Instructions of this type have been implemented in a number of systems, including microprocessors, such as the Motorola M68000 family (see Chapter 11).

A more general form of an atomic operation is the *Test And f* (TAf), where f(V,e) is an arithmetic or logical function of two values V and e [25]. A particular case of the TAf is the *Test And Add* (TAA) operation. It returns the value of V and replaces it with the value of the sum V + e. If we choose f to be a logic OR operation, and e = TRUE, then the TAf on (V,TRUE) is equivalent to the Test And Set (TAS) operation. The Test And Add is used on the NYU Ultracomputer for synchronization between numerous processors in an MIMD system (see Chapter 12).

3.4   Synchronization by Message Passing

An alternate method for synchronization between processes, running on separate processors, and in need of information exchange between them, is *message passing* [1, 3]. This is particularly applicable to *distributed* systems (loosely coupled), where there is no shared storage, although message passing can, in principle, be implemented in any system. The process transmitting the information is defined as the *sender*, and the process receiving it is the *receiver* [16]. Communication between processes is achieved by one process calling a procedure which is defined in the process with which it wishes to communicate. The parameter list of this procedure is used as a channel for the transfer of data between the processes.

Example: Process *sender* executes a command:

> *call* receiver.link (values, variables)

where process receiver contains a procedure declaration:

> *Proc* link (value parameters, result parameters)

The transmission of information is carried by the values specified by the sender and absorbed through the procedure link by the receiver.

In message passing, source and destination designators are names of processes [3]. Source and destination designators can also refer to global names or *mailboxes*.

One can have multiple client-server programs per mailbox. There are two basic approaches in message passing channel naming:

(a) *Static Channel Naming*—the source and destination designators are fixed at *compile time*.

(b) *Dynamic Channel Naming*—the source and destination designators are established at *run-time*.

In static channel naming, the programs may use only channels that are known at compile time. This limits their flexibility in a changing environment. It also implies that a process must have permanent access to a channel, even if it requires use of it for only a short period. In the dynamic channel naming, channels are treated as resources and allocated to processes when needed. Dynamic channel naming can be implemented with a static channel naming scheme that uses variables to contain source or destination designators.

An important issue in message passing is whether sending or receiving a message by a process, can introduce a delay in its further execution. A message statement that *never delays* the further execution of the invoking process, is called *nonblocking*. A message statement which may introduce a delay is called *blocking*. If there is no *buffer* between a sender and a receiver, both *send* and *receive* will be blocking and both the sender and the receiver will be delayed. If we use *buffered message passing*, the send might delay until there is enough room in the buffer. The receive might be delayed until there is a message in the buffer. We distinguish two cases:

(a) *Synchronous Message Passing*—no buffer between sender and receiver. Always blocking.

(b) *Asynchronous Message Passing* (send no-wait)—buffer assumed unbounded. The send is nonblocking.

Another way of message passing is through I/O commands [17]. Suppose we have two processes A and B, wishing to communicate. The procedure is as follows:

(a) An *Input* command in process A specifies as its source the name of another process B.

(b) An *Output* command in process B specifies as its destination the process A.

(c) The target variable of the input command matches the value denoted by the expression of the output command.

Sometimes, a process may require a certain service (such as running a given procedure) to be performed by another process, which may be running on a different processor. Such an operation is supported by a higher-level construct, called *Remote Procedure Call* [3]. The requesting process issues a statement of the following structure:

call server (value__arguments, results__arguments)

The name *server* may refer to the channel of transmission, the server (requested) process or to the type of service requested. The requested (server) process performs the service and returns the results to the requesting (client) process. The server process can be specified as follows:

> remote procedure server
> (in value__parameters; out result__parameters)
> body of the procedure
> end

After the server procedure is executed, the result values are passed to the client process via a *reply message*.

Alternately, the server process can be defined as a *statement*:

> accept server (in value__parameters; out result__parameters)

When this form is used, the remote procedure call is also called a *rendezvous*, because the client and the server processes meet for the execution of the accept statement and for passing the results from the server to the client.

3.5   Concurrent Languages

The concurrent programming languages can be classified into three basic categories [3]:

(a) *Procedure-oriented Languages* (POL) processes which have *direct access* to the *shared data* they want to manipulate. Mutual exclusion for critical sections must be ensured. Appropriate particularly for tightly coupled multiprocessors. Some examples are Concurrent Pascal and Modula.

(b) *Message-oriented Languages* (MOL) built upon primitive *send* and *receive* (see section 3.4). These processes, generally, do not have access to every data object. Every object has a caretaker process which manages it. In order to manipulate an object, a process must send a message to its caretaker. MOL can be implemented on both tightly and loosely coupled multiprocessors Some examples are Occam and Communicating Sequential Processes.

(c) *Operation-oriented Languages* (OOL) use the *remote procedure call* allowing a *client process* to call, by sending a message, upon a *server process*, which may or may not be on the same processor. The remote procedure call is the principal means for interprocess communication and synchronization. Operations are performed on objects by calling procedures as in POLs. Objects are managed by caretaker procedures as in MOLs. OOL can be implemented efficiently on multiprocessors and distributed systems (tightly or loosely coupled). Some examples are Ada and Distributed Processes.

Examples of some parallel programming languages will be briefly surveyed in the following discussion [1]. A detailed exposition of programming languages is outside the scope of this text.

Pascal Plus [18] is an extension of Pascal, similar in the parallel features that it offers to Concurrent Pascal [19] and Modula [20]. The parallel programming facilities of Pascal Plus are:

1. The *Process*, which is used to identify the parts of a program which may be executed in parallel.

2. The *Monitor* structure, which holds data shared by processes and guarantees that only one process at a time can modify that data (see section 3.3).

3. The *Condition*, which enables processes to synchronize their activities when using shared resources.

Processes in Pascal Plus represent independent actions which can execute in parallel. When they wish to compete for a shared variable or to cooperate on a task they must call a procedure of a monitor, which contains the shared data, protected by mutual exclusion. Conditions are used to identify queues of waiting processes. A process joins a queue by performing a *wait operation*; it remains on the queue until another process performs a *signal operation* (see section 3.3).

Modula-2 [21] features the *module* structure. It contains its own constants, variables, procedures, types, and import and export lists. A process in Modula-2 is implemented by means of a *coroutine* which is a set of local variables and statements specifying its activities. A coroutine is *created* by a call to a system procedure NEWPROCESS. It is *activated* by another system procedure TRANSFER. TRANSFER is used to identify within a coroutine explicit *scheduling points*, that is, the points at which one coroutine *resumes* another coroutine. A resumed coroutine continues execution in the same state as it was before it relinquished control. In this way control is transferred among the various processes of the system. High-level synchronization facilities can be implemented by using the program structuring tool, the *module*, and the signal type with its special WAIT and SEND operations. These facilities can be used to construct a module which simulates the function of a *monitor* with condition variables.

Ada [22, 23] was developed according to the specifications of the U.S. Department of Defense (Ada is a trademark of the U.S. Department of Defense), by the CII Honeywell Bull, France. The following features have been introduced in it:

1. *Readability*—particularly stressed over the ease of writing. Notation is explicit, including English-like constructs, to enhance documentation.

2. *Data Abstraction*—the details of data representation are kept separate from the specification of the logical operations on the data. In line with the developments introduced with Pascal.

3. *Strong Typing*—each variable explicitly declared and its type specified.

4. *Package*—a mechanism for encapsulation; enables a number of subprograms and the data which they manipulate to be grouped together and treated as a unit. Similar to the module of Modula-2. This can be compiled separately.

5. *Exception Handling*—the user is provided with a capability to specify what action to take if an error occurs.

6. *Generic Units*—a unit (such as a stack) can be defined independently of the type of objects it manipulates and the type can then be defined at a later time by the user.

7. *Tasking*—enables a program to be conceived as a series of *parallel* activities. This is one of the main features supporting concurrent programming.

A number of tasks can be declared in an Ada program. Different tasks proceed to execute independently and concurrently (if processors are available), communicating at points of synchronization. The communication approach in Ada is that one task calls a procedure defined in another task and the parameter list is used to provide for the transfer of data. In Ada the buffer between the sender and the receiver (see section 3.4) is represented as a task, accessed in a mutually exclusive manner. Only one task entry may be executing at a given time.

Occam [24] was developed by the Inmos Co. to be implemented on its single chip 32-bit microprocessors, the Transputers. The Transputers have been designed for an efficient configuration as a multiprocessor, as implemented for instance by the FPS Co. in its T-series, as described in Chapter 9.

The Occam uses the concept of a *process* to specify an action which can take place in parallel. There are three primitive processes:

1. *Assignment*—changes the value of a variable.
2. *Input*—receives a value from a channel.
3. *Output*—sends a value to a channel.

A *channel* is the means by which two processes can communicate with each other. A channel in Occam corresponds to a link on the transputer. By combining the above processes with the use of *constructors* a program in Occam is put together. There are three types of constructors:

(a) The *sequential constructor* (denoted by *seq*) (see section 3.2), causes its component processes to be executed sequentially, one after another, terminating when the last component terminates.

(b) The *parallel constructor* (denoted by *par*) causes its component processes to be executed concurrently, terminating when all its components are terminated.

(c) The *alternative constructor* (denoted by *alt*) chooses one of its component processes from among several processes for execution, terminating when the chosen component terminates.

There is also a *conditional process* which selects the first component process (whose Boolean expression is true) for execution and then terminates. A *repetitive process* which executes the component process for as long as the Boolean expression is true.

The transputer is a small but complete computer which can be used as a building block with other transputers to construct a distributed computer network. Each transputer has four I/O links which enable it to communicate with other transputers (the links are serial). When transputers are programmed in Occam each transputer implements an

Occam process and each link implements an Occam channel in each direction between two transputers. Processes in Occam cooperate with each other by passing messages directly over the channels (links). The range of features provided in Occam has been kept deliberately small, but sufficient enough to enable the specification of solutions to concurrent programming problems. These features map closely onto the transputer hardware, thereby increasing the efficiency of execution.

References   1. R. H. Perrott, *Parallel Programming*, Addison-Wesley, Reading, MA, 1987.

2. H. S. Stone, *High-performance Computer Architecture*, Addison-Wesley, Reading, MA, 1987 (Chapter 7).

3. M. J. Quinn, *Designing Efficient Algorithms for Parallel Computers*, McGraw-Hill, NY, 1987.

4. D. J. Kuck, *The Structure of Computers and Computations*, Vol. 1, John Wiley & Sons, NY, 1978.

5. M. Kallstrom, S. S. Thakkar, "Programming Three Parallel Computers," *IEEE Software*, Vol. 5, No. 1, pp. 11–22, Jan. 1988.

6. B. Kruatrachue, T. Lewis, "Grain Size Determination for Parallel Processing," *IEEE Software*, Vol. 5, No. 1, pp. 23–32, Jan. 1988.

7. M. J. Wolfe, "Multiprocessor Synchronization for Concurrent Loops," *IEEE Software*, Vol. 5, No. 1, pp. 34–42, Jan. 1988.

8. C. D. Polychronopoulos, "Compiler Optimizations for Enhancing Parallelism and their Impact on Architecture Design," *IEEE Trans. on Computers*, Vol. 37, No. 8, pp. 991–1004, Aug. 1988.

9. Z. Segall, L. Snyder, eds., "Proc. Workshop on Performance Efficient Parallel Programming," *Carnegie Mellon University Report*, CMU-CS-86-180, Sept. 1986.

10. D. A. Padua, M. J. Wolfe, "Advanced Compiler Optimizations for Supercomputers," *Comm. ACM*, Vol. 29, No. 12, pp. 1184–1201, Dec. 1986.

11. D. Gelernter, "Domesticating Parallelism," *IEEE Computer*, Vol. 19, No. 8, pp. 12–16, Aug. 1986.

12. K. Hwang, F. A. Briggs, *Computer Architecture and Parallel Processing*, McGraw-Hill, NY, 1984 (Chapter 7).

13. A. J. Bernstein, "Analysis of Programs for Parallel Processing," *IEEE Trans. on Computers*, Vol. C-15, pp. 746–757, Oct. 1966.

14. D. M. Ritchie, D. Thompson, "The UNIX Timesharing System," *Comm. ACM*, Vol. 17, No. 7, pp. 365–375, July 1974.

15. E. W. Dijkstra, *Cooperating Sequential Processes, in Programming Languages*, F. Genuys, ed., pp. 43–112, Academic Press, NY, 1968.

16. P. Brinch Hansen, "Distributed Processes: A Concurrent Programming Concept," *Comm. ACM*, Vol. 21, pp. 934–940, 1978.

17. C. A. R. Hoare, "Communicating Sequential Processes," *Comm. ACM*, Vol. 21, No. 8, pp. 666–677, Aug. 1978.

18. J. Welsh, D. W. Bustard, "Pascal Plus—Another Language for Modular Multiprogramming," *Software-practice and Experience*, Vol. 9, pp. 947–957, 1979.

19. P. Brinch Hansen, "The Programming Language Concurrent Pascal," *IEEE Trans. on Software Eng.*, Vol. 1, pp. 199–207, 1975.

20. N. Wirth, Modula: "A Language for Modular Multiprogramming," *Software—Practice and Experience*, Vol. 7, pp. 3–35, 1977.

21. N. Wirth, *Programming in Modula-2, 3rd. ed.*, Springer Verlag, NY, 1985.

22. J. G. P. Barnes, *Programming in Ada, 2nd. ed.*, Addison-Wesley, Reading, MA, 1984.

23. N. Gehani, Ada: *Concurrent Programming*, Prentice-Hall, Englewood Cliffs, NJ, 1984.

24. Inmos Ltd., *Occam Programming Manual*, Prentice-Hall, Englewood Cliffs, NJ, 1984.

25. A. Gottlieb, et al., "The NYU Ultracomputer—Designing an MIMD Shared Memory Parallel Computer," *IEEE Trans. on Computers*, Vol. C-32, No. 2, pp. 175–189, Feb. 1983.

CHAPTER 4

Multiprocessor Operating Systems

4.1 Multiprocessor OS Requirements

One of the primary tasks of an *Operating System* (OS) [1–5] is the efficient management of the shared resources of a computing system among a set of competing user programs. It can be viewed as an allocator of resources and an arbitrator between the demands of user programs which are subdivided into tasks and/or processes. The OS also manages the interface between different tasks or processes, between the system and the user, and between the processes and the I/O subsystems. The OS is a software entity consisting of a number of processes performing the following tasks:

- resource allocation (processors, I/O devices) to user programs;
- memory space allocation and management;
- execution of user programs;
- control and activation of I/O devices

and many others, depending on the particular properties of the computing system on which the OS is implemented.

A multiprocessor OS should support the concepts of *tasks* and *processes* as defined at the end of Chapter 1. The *task*, a basic unit of scheduling and allocation can be assigned to one or more *processors*. Any program may consist of a number of tasks. The creation of tasks within a program is one of the operations of the multiprocessor OS. Some of the other operations that the OS should be required to perform on tasks are termination, swapping in and out of different storage facilities, modification of address space size, migration from one region of physical store to another (or to a different system in distributed memory environment), state queries, and protection changes [5].

A task consists of one or more *processes* which are indivisible units with respect to allocation to run on a processor. The required OS operations on a process are creation, suspension, continuation, termination, scheduling, and group operations affecting all processes in a task [5]. The multiprocessor OS should provide an efficient *context switching* capability (a mechanism for rapidly switching the attention of a *processor* from one *process* to another) [2]. Sharing processors among a number of processes introduces further requirements from the OS:

    (a) The *protection* of the resources of one process from any interference by other processes.

(b) The provision of *communication* among processes. Particularly providing for message passing and shared memory communication facilities (critical sections and semaphores).

(c) The *allocation* of resources among processes so that resource demands can always be fulfilled.

A multiprocessor OS should be designed as a multiple-user facility. It should support memory hierarchies directly and it should provide efficient management of cache, main memory and secondary storage. It should include special facilities to deal with the problems of *coherence* between different storage modules (cache coherence will be discussed later in Chapter 5). In addition to the specific multiprocessor requirements, the OS should, of course, support all regular OS tasks existing in any uniprocessor (such as user registration on a computing system and accounting and management of both batch and interactive use, file management). The OS should above all be *reliable* and be able to continue to operate correctly in the presence of user errors [1–5].

An OS is usually subdivided into two basic parts:

1. *Kernel* contains the principal, critical routines to manage resources and perform other tasks, mentioned above. It should be protected from overwriting.

2. *Utility routines* are subprograms linked with ordinary tasks or special purpose tasks, built by system programmers [5].

The realization of multiprocessor OS is discussed in the next section.

4.2 Multiprocessor OS Realization

There are a number of possible organizations for implementing OS in a multiprocessor system [2]:

(a) *Master-slave organization*. One of the processors is selected to be a *Master*; it always executes the OS. Other processors are denoted as *Slaves*. If a slave processor needs any OS service it must request it and wait until the current program, running on the master, is interrupted. This may introduce some idle time for the slave processors. The entire system is subject to catastrophic failures; failure of the master will certainly be such. An advantage of this organization is its relative software and hardware simplicity. It is most effective for special applications where the workload is well defined or for asymmetrical systems in which the slaves have less capability than the master processor. Some implementation examples are CDC Cyber 170 and DEC 10.

(b) *Separate OS organization*. The OS kernel is run separately on each processor. Many of the routines exist in a number of copies which are distributed among the processors' local storage. Although the system is less prone to catastrophic failures, it wastes too much storage keeping multiple copies of routines and data. This organization is more suitable for loosely coupled distributed systems.

(c) *Floating OS organization.* The Master assignment "floats" from one processor to another. There is also a possibility that several of the processors may be executing OS routines at the same time. A better load balancing among processors can be attained in this organization. This organization is more complicated to implement, but it is more flexible and reliable as compared to the Master-Slave organization. In case of failures, graceful degradation of the system is possible; a failure of any single processor is usually not catastrophic. Examples of implementation are MVS and VM OS in IBM3081 and Hydra in Carnegie Mellon C.mmp.

The basic software unit that the OS manages is the *process* (the indivisibly scheduled unit on a separate processor). As the computing system operates under the OS management, new processes are created. While others are terminated, some processes are running on processors while some are temporarily inactive. We can distinguish the following *process states* [3]:

1. *New*—just created by the OS.
2. *Ready*—waiting to be assigned to a processor.
3. *Running*—having its instructions executed by the processor assigned to it.
4. *Blocked*—a running process waiting for some event, such as an I/O completion, to occur.
5. *Halted*—is inactive and execution has been stopped. It is not waiting for an imminent processor assignment. The execution may have been stopped either because it was completed, or because of some fatal error.

Each process is represented in the OS by its own *Process Control Block* (PCB) or *Process State Descriptor* (PSD) which is sometimes simply called the *Process Context*. The PCB is a data block or record containing information associated with a specific process including:

- *Process State* can be new, ready, running, blocked, or halted.
- *Program Counter* indicates the address of the next instruction of the process to be executed.
- *CPU Registers* contents. The list of registers saved for each PCB will vary on different systems with different architectures.
- *Memory Management Information* includes base and bounds registers or page tables.
- *Accounting Information* includes the amount of CPU and real time used, time limits, account numbers, job, or process numbers.
- *I/O Status Information* includes outstanding I/O requests, I/O devices allocated to this process, and a list of open files.
- *CPU Scheduling Information* includes process priority and pointers to scheduling queues.
- *Protection Information* includes the process status in the protection hierarchy, if any.

The above list may change in size and content between different systems. In any system, the PCB serves as the respository of information that may vary from process to process.

Suppose a process A is running on a processor. For some reason the OS interrupts process A in order to run process B on the same processor (it can occur if process B has a higher priority than A and no other processor can be allocated, for instance). This is when a *context switch* occurs. The current information, associated with process A will be stored in the appropriate locations of its PCB (contents of PC and CPU registers, among other information), so that process A could be restarted later on without repeating any instructions already executed. After the above storage, the values of PC, CPU registers and others from the PCB of process B, are moved into the appropriate locations in the CPU and process B starts running on the processor.

4.3   Deadlock

The processes in a multiprocessor system compete for the use of a limited number of resources (such as I/O interface channels). It may happen that a number of processes hold a number of resources, while other processes, which have a need to use the same resources, are blocked. Such an event is called *deadlock* [2–4]. A deadlock may occur as a result of one or more of the following conditions:

(a) *Mutual Exclusion*—when each process claims exclusive control of the resources allocated to it.

(b) *Nonpreemption*—when a process cannot release the resources it holds until they are used to completion.

(c) *Wait For*—when processes hold resources already allocated to them while waiting for additional resources.

(d) *Circular Wait*—when each process holds one or more resources that are being requested by the next process in a circular chain of processes.

There are a number of approaches to solve the deadlock problem.

1. *Prevention*. Processes are constrained in such a way that requests for use of resources leading to a deadlock never occur. The OS is designed in such a way so that the above conditions for deadlock (a), (b), (c), or (d) never hold. The scheduler procedure of the OS allocates resources to processes so that deadlocks will never occur. Empirical observations indicate that deadlock prevention mechanisms tend to overcommit resources.

2. *Avoidance*. The scheduler procedure of the OS controls resource allocation to processes on the basis of advance information about expected resource usage so that deadlock is avoided. Avoidance tends to overcommit resources to a smaller degree than prevention. Blocking situations, however, may still arise and waiting time of some processes may be increased while other processes take hold of the resources somewhat earlier than necessary.

3. *Detection*. The OS uses the information in the processes' PCBs to detect whether or not a deadlock exists. Having detected an existing deadlock, the OS proceeds with the next step of recovery.

4. *Recovery*. In order to break a deadlock, the OS must release at least one resource from one of the processes even if its use has not been completed. The process which has been interrupted in its use of the resource should later be *restored* to permit an orderly use of the above resource. This is accomplished through a *rollback* mechanism which is provided by the OS [2].

4.4 Distributed OS

In tightly coupled multiprocessors with shared memory, synchronization can be realized both through data values, residing in the shared memory (such as semaphores), as well as by message passing. In loosely coupled, distributed computing systems, the memory is distributed among the processors and the nodes of the system. In other words, we have basically local memory assigned to each processor. The OS must, therefore, rely more heavily on the communication capability between the nodes in distributed systems. In distributed systems the design of the OS is closely related to the design of the *communication network* of the system [3]. The following issues should be addressed in this design:

(a) *Routing strategies*—how is information, messages, sent through the network?

(b) *Connection strategies*—how do two (or more) processes establish an interconnection between them?

(c) *Contention*—how should conflicting demands by a number of processes for the same resource be resolved?

(d) *Structure*—what are the major components, organization, and the configuration of the communication network?

The above issues will be discussed in the following.

In a distributed system there may be a number of possible paths to send a message between any two nodes. The OS of each node contains a *routing table*, indicating the alternative paths that can be used to send a message to other nodes. The table may include cost and transmission speed information, and it may be updated as necessary. We can distinguish the following *routing* policies:

1. *Fixed routing*. A path between any two nodes is specified in advance and remains fixed. Usually the shortest path is chosen. This is an unflexible method, unadaptable to load changes in various paths of the communication network. Unnecessary delays may be caused by not using alternate, possibly less busy, paths.

2. *Virtual circuit*. A path between two nodes is fixed for the duration of one communication session. Different sessions between the same pair of nodes may involve different paths. This method is much more flexible than the fixed routing.

3. *Dynamic routing*. The path to send a message between two nodes is chosen only when a message is sent. Separate messages (even in the same session) may be

assigned different paths. Usually, a link in the path, which is least used, is chosen. This method is the most flexible, however, allowing messages of the same session to arrive out of order. (In the previous methods messages arrive in the same order in which they were sent.) This can be remedied by appending a sequence number to each message.

The most common *connection strategies* are:

1. *Circuit switching*. A *permanent link* between two processes is established for the duration of the communication between the processes. No other process can use that link during that time. This is similar to the telephone system and requires more setup time.

2. *Message switching*. A *temporary link* between two processes is established for the duration of one message transfer. This is similar to the mailing of letters by the post office. Many messages, from different users, can be transmitted over the same link. This yields a higher system utilization of the communication network and requires less setup time.

3. *Packet switching*. Messages are subdivided in fixed-length parts called *packets*. A message may consist of one or any number of packets. Each packet may be sent to its destination separately over a different path. The packets are reassembled into messages upon arrival at the destination. More overhead per message is required in this method.

The same link in a communication network may be used in the interconnection path between a number of pairs of nodes. Thus, *contention* over the use of the same link may arise when a number of accesses are attempted simultaneously. There are several techniques to deal with this problem.

1. *Collision detection*. Before sending a message over a link, the node OS probes and checks whether the link is busy. If the link is busy and no other is available, the node OS enters a wait state, checking the availability of the link periodically. The method tends to prevent collisions between messages over the same link, but on the other hand, performance is degraded due to numerous wait states when the system is busy. This approach has been successfully used in the Ethernet system.

2. *Token passing*. The OS generates a special unique message, called a *token*, continuously circulating among the nodes of the system (usually, in this case, the nodes are interconnected in a ring structure). A node which wants to transmit, removes the token from the network, when it arrives, and begins to send its messages. When the transmission is complete, the node retransmits the token. If the token gets lost, a node OS must be able to detect it and generate a new token. In a distributed system, there must be preprogrammed in the OS, an *election* algorithm [3], which establishes the node which regenerates the token and starts it going again. A token passing scheme has been implemented by Primenet.

3. *Message slots*. A number of fixed length message slots continuously circulate in the system (usually a ring structure). Each slot can hold a fixed-size message along with some control information such as source, destination, slot empty, or slot full.

When an empty slot arrives, a node inserts its message along with the appropriate control information. When the full slot arrives at the destination node (the destination encoding is checked at each node where the slot arrives), the message is unloaded and the slot is set to empty and recirculated in the system. A new message may be inserted by the receiving node, if it is ready to transmit. Since the slots are of fixed size, some messages may be broken down into smaller packets, fitting the slot size. This method has been implemented in the Cambridge Digital Communication Ring.

There exists an International Standards Organization (ISO) which works on establishing different standards, particularly for computer communication. The ISO has proposed to represent the *structure* of a distributed computer communication system as a hierarchy of seven layers. The ISO layers are:

1. *Physical layer*—responsible for handling the mechanical and electrical details of the physical transmission of a bit stream.
2. *Data link layer*—responsible for handling the packets, including any error detection and recovery that occurred in the physical layer.
3. *Network layer*—responsible for providing connections and routing packets in the communication network, including the handling and decoding of packet addresses and maintaining routing information for proper response to changing loads.
4. *Transport layer*—responsible for low-level access to the network and the transfer of messages between the nodes, including partitioning messages into packets, maintaining packet order, flow control, and physical address generation.
5. *Session layer*—responsible for implementing the process-to-process protocols.
6. *Presentation layer*—responsible for resolving the differences in formats among the various nodes in the network.
7. *Application layer*—responsible for interfacing directly with the users. Deals with electronic mail and distributed data bases.

Not all of these seven layers may explicitly exist in each and every system. In some systems, a number of layers and their tasks may be merged into a single layer.

The geographic distribution of the nodes of a distributed system has an influence on its OS design [3]. The distance between the nodes of a *computer network* [6] are generally large. For instance, the Arpanet is distributed over the whole of the United States. Typical links in a computer network are telephone lines, microwave links, and satellite channels. Such links are relatively slow and have a low reliability figure. They are controlled by special *communication processors* which interface between the processor nodes and the network. On the other hand, *local area networks* (LAN) are distributed over a relatively small area, such as a single building or a number of adjacent buildings. The communication links, in this case coaxial cable and fiber optics, have a higher speed and reliability and a lower error rate as compared to computer networks. The above differences in speed and error probability should be reflected in the OS design for the above types of systems.

Each node in a distributed system maintains its own local *file* system. When a user at a given node, say A, accesses a file located in A's storage, the OS handles it as any regular file access on a single-computing system. When a user at node A has a need to access a file located at another node, there are two basic approaches for file management by the OS of a distributed system [3]:

(a) *The Centralized Approach.* All *shared files* (shared among different nodes) reside at a single, centralized node called a *file server*. From the node OS standpoint, there are *local* and *non-local files*. However, the location of the files is transparent to the user; local and non-local files are accessed in the same manner by the user. The node OS differentiates between the two types of files. It converts accesses to shared non-local files into messages to the file server, which transfers the file to the user's node. This method is prone to bottlenecks around the file server. An example of implementation is the Network File System (NFS) of Sun Microsystems.

(b) *The Distributed Approach.* Any file at any node can be accessed by any node in the system. In some applications the file location (node of residence address) must be included in the file access request. In other implementations, the file location may be transparent to the user. In this case the OS must maintain tables which allow it to find a file anywhere in the network.

One of the main advantages of a distributed system is its fault tolerance. The computing devices (processors) and memory are distributed among a number of nodes. If a failure occurs at a certain node, other nodes can continue functioning. In order for the whole system to proceed with its work, despite partial failure, the OS has to be equipped with features permitting the *detection* and *isolation* of failure spots. Subsequently, the OS should be able to manage the *reconfiguration* of the communication network, to avoid routing of messages through a faulty node.

After the node has been repaired, the OS should be able to manage the *recovery* of the system by *integrating* the former faulty resource back into the system [3]. The detection process can be enhanced by the design of test handshaking protocols to be exchanged on a periodic basis between the nodes of the system. A break in the protocol, that is, failure to receive specific control signals at an appropriate time will indicate a possible breakdown. The reconfiguration capability should be supported by appropriate hardware facilities featuring software-controlled switches, which can change the system's interconnection configuration. An example of such a reconfigurable computer communication system is described in [7].

4.5 Examples of Multiprocessor OS

4.5.1 Carnegie Mellon C.mmp Hydra

The Hydra is an experimental OS kernel developed at the Carnegie Mellon University for the C.mmp multiprocessor [2, 8]. The C.mmp multiprocessor has 16 processors (DEC PDP-11/40E) and 16 memory modules (for a total of 32 MBytes shared memory), connected by a 16x16 crossbar switch. Each processor has 8 BKytes local memory and I/O devices, connected to its local Unibus (a trademark of DEC).

The Hydra is an *object-oriented system*. All information in the system is encapsulated in software structures called *objects* which are accessed only through *capabilities*. Thus, Hydra has also *capability-based protection mechanism*. The Intel 432 system was also object-oriented with capability-based protection and designed for multiprocessing implementation [9]. Objects contain information of the same type. The set of objects which a process can access is called its *address space*. The objects are of variable size and consist of a data part and a capability list (called the *C list*). The data part of an object consists of two components:

(a) *representation* which contains the actual information; and

(b) *type* indicating the nature of the information.

The C list consists of a set of capabilities. A process may only perform those operations on an object that are permitted by the *access rights* in the capability through which the process named the object.

The basic unit of a schedulable entity in Hydra is a *process*. An active process may migrate from one processor to another; it is not bound to any specific processor. The set of objects defined by the capabilities of a process at a given time defines the execution environment and the protection environment of the process. The record of the execution environment of a process is called the *Local Name Space* (LNS), an object type.

A *procedure* object contains a list of references to other objects which must be accessed during the execution of the procedure's code. There is a unique LNS for each invocation of the procedure. This LNS disappears after the procedure terminates its execution.

System *interrupts* are provided to facilitate interprocessor communication. The Hydra provides a *message* system which uses objects called *ports* as gateways for processes to send and receive messages between each other. Each port has a set of logical terminals called *channels* which are used to connect between sender and receiver processes. Messages are sent from *output channels* and received in *input channels*. Two processes can communicate if they each have a capability for the other's port and if a communication path is established between the ports.

In addition to the messages mechanism, the Hydra also uses *locks* and *semaphores* (see Chapter 3) for synchronization. There are two types of locks on Hydra:

(a) *Kernel lock*—makes use of the hardware facilities such as interprocessor interrupts, which are not available to the user. Used primarily to provide mutual exclusion for operations on various system queues and tables.

(b) *Spin lock*—available to the users. No privileged instructions are used to implement it.

Although the Hydra was implemented on an experimental system (C.mmp) it was an innovative multiprocessor OS and its principles are implemented in many other systems. It certainly had a strong impact and influence on the development of multiprocessor operating systems.

4.5.2 IBM Multiprocessors OS

The IBM Corporation has developed a number of multiprocessing systems in its 360–370 family which were initiated in the mid-1960s and still actively continued [2, 10, 11]. For instance, the 370/168MP and the 3081 were dual processors, the 3084 had four processors and the latest, 3090, can be configured with up to six processors [11]. IBM has extended its System 370 OS to operate in a multiprocessing environment. In fact, more than one OS is featured on the IBM multiprocessors.

The most notable IBM multiprocessor OS is the MVS/XA, an extension of the OS/360 [12]. It implements the Floating OS organization (see section 4.2), where the OS can execute on any of the system processors, none of which is identified as a permanent master. The programs, running in the MVS/XA environment, are identified as *jobs*. Each job runs in its own *address space*. Within the overall storage (up to 2 GBytes) the MVS/XA establishes a *Common Storage Area* (CSA), accessible by any program in the system. The CSA can be used to implement Remote Procedure Calls [13], where one program leaves a request for another program in a prearranged part of the common area, and returns later to pick up the results of its request. Each job in the system has its own *private area* within the overall storage.

The MVS/XA is designed to manage multitasking. When a job begins execution the MVS/XA sets up a *Task Control Block* to describe the running program. The running task is provided by the MVS/XA with the capability to start up *subtasks* with adjustable priorities. The *task* is the smallest schedulable unit of work recognized by the MVS/XA. Tasks can be scheduled to run in parallel on available processors. They all *share*, however, the same address space of up to 2 GBytes. The MVS/XA also supports a *Dual Address Space* capability, where a program can access information in either its own address space or in a *secondary* address space. This extends the effective address space to 4 GBytes (32-bit address). This concept is extended in a projected MVS/XA superset called *MVS/Enterprise Systems Architecture* [14]. It allows the user to specify up to 8192(8K) secondary address spaces up to a total of 16 Terabytes (2**44 Bytes). Several cooperating programs, running in different address spaces, may share access to a common address space.

The MVS/XA supports the *reconfigurability* of the multiprocessors on which it is implemented. This capability permits reassignment of resources between a number of subsystems of the multiprocessor. The reconfigurable components under the MVS/XA are [12]:

1. Processors;
2. Storage modules;
3. Channel (I/O) paths; and
4. I/O devices.

A reconfiguration under MVS/XA may involve adding or removing some of the above components from the overall system configuration. Some of the reasons for a reconfiguration operation are:

(a) Malfunction of a component and its subsequent replacement.

(b) Maintenance to be performed on some of the components.

(c) A change in workload, necessitating the reconfiguring of a single system into two separate systems, or transferring components from one subsystem to another.

The MVS/XA features CONFIG and VARY commands, specifying which elements to configure and whether they are to be made online or offline to the system. Reconfiguration processing has two stages:

1. *Logical reconfiguration* which makes the component online or offline to MVS/XA. The process involves marking entries in MVS/XA system resource tables.

2. *Physical reconfiguration* which makes the component online or offline to the hardware. This process often involves the setting of hardware switches that control whether access to the component is physically possible.

Both logical and physical reconfiguration are performed by the MVS/XA reconfiguration command processor. The *CONFIG command* also allows the operator to display which hardware components are presently online to the system and which items are available to be configured online or offline.

The MVS/XA software and the system hardware provide support for *interprocessor communication* (IPC). To accomplish this communication, MVS/XA uses the *signal processor* (SIGP) instruction. A SIGP instruction signals a processor and transmits a request to perform a function. The addressed processor decodes the request, performs the requested function (if possible), and transmits a response to the calling processor. The response contains a condition code and status information. Some of the purposes of the above communication, under MVS/XA, are:

1. System initialization.

2. Dispatch (assign) work to another processor.

3. Stop or restart a processor during reconfiguration.

4. Attempt alternate CPU recovery for a processor failure due to a software malfunction. As part of recovery processing, the functioning processor might issue SIGP instructions to determine the status of the failing processor. If the status can be obtained, the MVS/XA recovery routines have a better chance of succeeding.

An alternate OS available on IBM multiprocessors, particularly the 3090 system, is the VM [15, 16]:

• VM/SP—HPO (*High-performance Option*) providing improvements in throughput and response time on multiprocessors with a large number of components; and

• *VM/XA System Facility* providing the capability of running multiple OS ("guest" OS) on the same system.

The IBM experimental multiprocessor RP3 [17] operates both under a modified BSD 4.2 UNIX [3] and under an experimental IBM VM/EPEX environment. VM/EPEX is an extension of VM/SP.

4.5.3 Multiprocessor Extensions of Unix

The Unix OS is organized in layers [3, 18, 19]. The innermost layer is the *kernel* which interfaces directly with the hardware and is responsible for implementing the *file* and *process* abstractions. Surrounding the kernel are various layers of user-accessible programs. The innermost user-program layer obtains services from the kernel via a system-call interface. Programs in the outer layer employ other user programs as building blocks and, therefore, interface with the kernel indirectly.

The *file* and the *process* are the key concepts of the Unix kernel. Unix files are organized in a dynamic, hierarchical structure of directories and they may be manipulated by a small set of operations, such as opening or closing a file and reading or writing some bytes into the file. A Unix *process* can be considered a virtual computer, including memory, access to devices, and a way to execute instructions. Processes can both replicate themselves and communicate with each other via *pipes* or, in some variants of Unix, via *sockets*. Using pipes and *shell scripts* (programs written in the language of the command interpreter), also called *application programs* or *commands*, one can create new programs and interact with the kernel via system calls. The shell scripts are structured as ordinary user programs and can be substituted by the user with alternate software.

Some of the main requirements, posed in the extension of Unix to multiprocessors, are [19]:

1. Provide for mutual exclusion primitives (see section 3.3).
2. Provide for synchronization capabilities (see sections 3.4 and 4.1).
3. Provide for multiprocessor task scheduling capability (see section 4.2).
4. Provide for efficient interprocess communication (see sections 3.4 and 4.1).
5. Provide flexible memory management capability and cache coherency (see Chapter 5).
6. Provide for easy reconfigurability and expandability (see subsection 4.5.2).

A recent extension of Unix (Unix 4.3BSD) designed to manage a multiprocessing environment is the *Mach* OS, developed at the Carnegie-Mellon University and funded by DARPA [19–21]. Mach has four fundamental abstractions:

(a) *Port*—a queue or a communication channel for messages, protected by the kernel. All communication traffic within Mach makes references to ports as read or write destinations using the primitives *Send* and *Receive* (see section 3.4).

(b) *Task*—contains the resources associated with a process (address space, file descriptors, port-access capabilities). Does not perform computations itself, but serves as a framework in which *threads* can operate.

(c) *Thread*—control unit most basic to CPU utilization, containing the minimal processing state associated with a computation—a program counter, a stack pointer, and other hardware register state information. A *Unix process* corresponds to a Mach *task* containing a *single thread*. A Mach task may contain multiple threads, but each thread is associated with exactly one task. Multiple threads within a task may execute in parallel. A thread can also be termed as a *lightweight process*.

(d) *Message*—consists of a fixed-length header and a typed collection of data objects used in communication between threads. A message can be of any size and may contain port-access capabilities in addition to data.

In addition to message passing, Mach also implements shared memory techniques (see Chapter 3). Mach's *virtual memory system* features read/write and copy-on-write sharing of memory between tasks. It is structured around four data types:

1. *Address map*—describes the regions of memory that comprise the task's address space. Every region refers to either a *virtual memory object* or *share map*.

2. *Virtual memory object*—represents the backing storage for a memory region. It maintains information as to what pages of the object are currently resident and where to find nonresident pages.

3. *Share map*—provides a level of indirection above the virtual memory objects, thereby allowing the same memory object to be shared by multiple tasks.

4. *Resident page*—used to keep track of the state of the machine's physical pages (free, reclaimable, in use, in which virtual memory object).

Mach's interprocessor communication messages may contain collections of ports, port access rights, and other data. A *copy-on-write* method to pass messages is used. The only time data are actually copied, not just pointed to, is when either the sender or receiver attempts to modify the data. In such an event, only a copy of the modified page of data is made. The remainder of the data buffer continues to be shared. This method tends to lower the overhead (see Chapter 2).

The Carnegie Mellon Mach OS has been ported by the BBN Corporation to its GP1000 Butterfly system (see section 10.1).

An extension of the AT&T Unix System V, the UNICOS [22], has been implemented on the following Cray systems:

• CRAY 1 (4 processors);

• CRAY Y-MP

• CRAY X-MP and

• CRAY 1.

Like the AT&T Unix the UNICOS is written in C. The kernel of UNICOS has been enhanced in the area of I/O processing, the use of very large data files, multiprocessing support, and user multitasking. The most visible of the UNICOS utilities is the command interpreter, called the *shell*. The shell is a high-level programming language that provides a customized user interface. The shell functions as another user process. Shell programming is accomplished through the use of *shell scripts*, which allow users to group command lines into a file for a single-command execution. Shell scripts are analogous to IBM *Job Control Language* (JCL) procedure files.

4.5.4   The V Distributed System OS

The *V Distributed System OS* [23] was developed for a cluster of computer workstations connected by a high-performance network. The system is structured as a *distributed kernel*, a set of service modules, various run-time libraries, and a set of commands. The kernel is distributed in the sense that a separate copy of the kernel executes on each participating network node. However the separate copies of the kernel cooperate to provide a single-system abstraction of processes in address spaces, communicating using a base set of communication primitives. The existence of multiple resources and network interconnection is largely transparent at the process level. The service modules implement value-added services using the basic access to hardware resources provided by the kernel. For instance, the V-file server implements a Unix-like file system using the raw disk access supported by the kernel.

The memory in distributed systems is usually local with each node and not shared (see section 4.4). However, shared memory is the most natural way for storing information (shared among a number of nodes). Shared memory can be implemented across multiple node processors by caching references data as virtual memory pages and implementing a *consistency* protocol between the page frame caches on different nodes. The V Distributed System designers have been investigating efficient mechanisms for implementing consistency between network nodes such as software structuring techniques that reduce contention and cost called *problem-oriented shared memory*.

The V system also supports the *multicast* capability for sending information to a specific *subset* of the hosts or processes, as opposed to *broadcast*, which is sending to *all* hosts or processes in the network.

The V kernel provides software support for network-transparent abstraction of address spaces, processes and interprocess communication (IPC). The IPC facility provides a fast transport-level service for remote procedure calls, as characterized by file read and write operations. A *Send* primitive is implemented. The *Kernel Servers* encompass time, process, memory, communication and device management in addition to the basic communication facilities. Each of these functions is implemented by a separate kernel module that is replicated in each host node, handling the local processes, address spaces and devices. Each module is registered with the IPC facility and invoked from the process level using the standard IPC resources, the same as if the module executed outside the kernel as a process.

The *Kernel Process Server* implements operations to create, destroy, query, modify, and migrate processes. The *Kernel Memory Management Server* supports demand paging and provides memory protection by encapsulation in virtual address spaces. An address space consists entirely of ranges of addresses, called *regions*, bound to some portion of an open file.

The V has been implemented in a network consisting of VAX and Sun workstations [23].

References 1. M. Joseph, V. R. Prasad, N. Natarajan, *A Multiprocessor Operating System*, Prentice-Hall, Englewood Cliffs, NJ, 1984.

2. K. Hwang, F. A. Briggs, *Computer Architecture and Parallel Processing*, McGraw-Hill, NY, 1984.

3. A. Silberschatz, J. L. Peterson, *Operating System Concepts*, *alternate ed.*, Addison Wesley, Reading, MA, 1988.

4. R. W. Turner, *Operating Systems Design and Implementation*, Macmillan, NY, 1986.

5. D. Black et al., "Operating System Characteristics, Proc. Workshop on Performance-Efficient Parallel Programming," *Carnegie-Mellon Univ. Report CMV-CS-86-180*, pp. 9–12, Sept. 1986.

6. J. S. Quarterman, J. C. Hoskins, "Notable Computer Networks," *Comm. ACM*, Vol. 29, No. 10, pp. 932–971, Oct. 1986.

7. J. Etkin, D. Tabak, "Microcomputer-embedded Distributed Control of a Switching and Communication System," in *Microprocessor-based Control Systems*, N. K. Sinha, ed., pp. 343–367, D. Reidel Publishing G., Dordrecht, The Netherlands, 1986.

8. W. A. Wulf, R. Levin, S. P. Harbison, *HYDRA/C.mmp: An Experimental Computer System*, McGraw-Hill, NY, 1981.

9. E. I. Organick, *A Programmer's View of the Intel 432 System*, McGraw-Hill, NY, 1983.

10. D. Gifford, A. Spector, "Case Study: IBM's System/360–370 Architecture," *Comm. ACM*, Vol. 30, No. 4, pp. 292–307, April 1987.

11. S. G. Tucker, "The IBM 3090 System: An Overview," *IBM Systems Journal*, Vol. 25, No. 1, pp. 4–19, 1986.

12. "MVS/Extended Architecture Overview," *IBM Corp. Report GC28–1348*.

13. M. J. Quinn, *Designing Efficient Algorithms for Parallel Computers*, McGraw-Hill, NY, 1987.

14. "MVS/Enterprise System Architecture," *IBM Announcement No. 288–059*.

15. Y. Singh, G. M. King, J. W. Anderson, "IBM 3090 Performance: A Balanced System Approach," *IBM Systems Journal*, Vol. 25, No. 1, pp. 20–35, 1986.

16. M. C. Enichen, D. R. Patterson, "VM/SP: Introduction to Multiprocessing Concepts," *IBM Report GG22–9247*, Sept. 1981.

17. G. F. Pfister et al., "The IBM Research Parallel Processor Prototype (RP3): Introduction and Architecture," *Proc. 1985 Int. Conf. on Parallel Processing*, pp. 764–771, St. Charles, IL, Aug. 1985.

18. D. M. Ritchie, K. Thompson, "The Unix Time-Sharing System," *Comm. ACM*, Vol. 17, No. 7, pp. 365–375, July 1974.

19. C. H. Russell, P. J. Waterman, "Variations on Unix for Parallel-Processing Computers," *Comm. ACM*, Vol. 30, No. 12, pp. 1048–1055, Dec. 1987.

20. R. Rashid, "Threads of a New System," *Unix Review*, Vol. 4, No. 8, pp. 37–49, Aug. 1986.

21. R. Rashid et al., "Machine-independent Virtual Memory Management for Paged Uniprocessor and Multiprocessor Architectures," *IEEE Trans. on Computers*, Vol. 37, No. 8, pp. 896–908, Aug. 1988.

22. "UNICOS Operating System for Cray Supercomputers," *Cray Research Inc. Document CCMP-1102*, 1988.

23. D. R. Cheriton, "The V Distributed System," *Comm. ACM*, Vol. 31, No. 3, pp. 314–333, March 1988.

CHAPTER 5

Problems of Multiprocessor Design

Research and development of multiprocessor systems has been a very active area for many years. There are a number of problems in the design of multiprocessor systems, some of which are still being studied and researched [1, 2]. Some aspects of the above problems have been discussed in the previous chapters.

One of the important problems of multiprocessor design is the establishment of a scheduling policy [1]. *Scheduling* is the allocation of *jobs* or *tasks* or *processes* (see chapter 1) to the available hardware resources such as processors or I/O interfaces. Two basic scheduling approaches can be distinguished:

(a) *Static* scheduling performed by the user during the algorithm design stage or at compile time by the compiler. For instance, the Occam language (see section 3.5) allows programmers to specify the instruction execution sequence, the channel of communication, and the execution unit. While applying the static approach, scheduling costs are paid only once, no matter how many times the program is run with different data. There is no run-time overhead due to scheduling. On the other hand, it is difficult to predict exactly the run time profile of each task and this may cause some inefficiency in the allocation assignments and in the utilization of resources.

(b) *Dynamic* scheduling performed by the machine at run time. It offers possible better utilization of resources, at the price of additional scheduling time (at each run). The dynamic scheduling algorithm can be:

    (1) *Centralized*, performed by a fixed scheduler at all times. A performance bottleneck may develop for a large number of processors.

    (2) *Distributed*, where tasks, specified by the user at algorithm time, are put into a central queue in the shared memory at run time. Each available processor takes the first task from the queue and executes it. Bottlenecks can be avoided by designing a mechanism allowing simultaneous access from all processors to the same memory location without performance degradation, as implemented in the NYU Ultracomputer [3].

No less important than scheduling is the problem of *synchronization*, the management of the order of execution of different processes in different processors, particularly when some processors depend on the results attained by other processes, running on other processors. This entails the design of efficient passing of information between processes, either by the use of *shared memory* or by direct *message-passing* (see section

3.4). One has to design an efficient *communication* system, with minimal blocking, in order to support the above information transmission capabilities (see Chapter 2). Efficient handling of critical sections and mutual exclusion algorithms (see section 3.3) also contributes to the enhancement of the synchronization mechanism in a multiprocessor system.

In a multiprocessor system we have a number of processors and memory modules. There is a problem of *memory latency*—the time between the issuing of a memory access request (read or write) by a processor and the completion of the access operation [4]. Naturally, the designer should strive to minimize the memory latency. The use of an efficient interconnection network, such as in the BBN Butterfly (see Chapters 2 and 10), goes a long way to reduce memory latency.

Each individual processor in a multiprocessing system may have its own cache. In such a system, the memory scheme is composed of the main memory (shared in tightly coupled systems) and a number of individual cache memories. The same information may reside in a number of copies in the main memory and in some of the caches. In order to ensure the ability of the system to execute memory operations correctly, the above multiple copies should be kept identical. This brings us to the *memory*, or *cache-coherence* problem [2]. A memory scheme is *coherent* if the value returned on a load instruction is always the value given by the latest store instruction with the same address [5].

Cache incoherence can be caused by a number of events [2]. Consider a multiprocessor in which each individual processor has its own private cache. Two or more processors may be using the same data structure S, a copy of which is located in the shared main memory and in each one of the caches. If one of the processors (say A) performs a write operation into S in its cache, its copy will be different from the one in the main memory or in the cache of another processor (say B). If a *write-through* cache policy is implemented, the memory copy will be immediately updated, but not the copy in the cache of processor B. If a *write-back* policy is implemented, the memory copy will not be updated until the whole block in cache containing the modified location, is replaced and returned to the main memory. In either case, we have a memory inconsistency or incoherence.

In some multiprocessors *process migration* is allowed. In this case, a process may be scheduled to run on more than one processor during its lifetime. If process A, running on processor P0 modified data in the structure S and in the cache of P0, and is then migrated to processor P1 before the main memory has been updated, an inconsistency may arise. This will happen if process A attempts to load data from S to processor P1 before the main memory has been updated. The contents of S in the memory and the cache of P1 will be different from that in the cache of P0. This is another case of memory incoherence.

Another event that may cause memory incoherence is I/O *Direct Memory Access* (DMA) activity. In the case of input, the main memory would be accessed and updated, but not the cache (if the DMA modified locations which also reside in the cache). In the case of output occurring before the memory locations have been updated (write-back policy), stale data may be transmitted to the output device. I/O-based memory incoherence can be overcome by making the *I/O Processor* (IOP) a participant in the cache coherence protocol, and be adopted in the system.

There exist a number of approaches to solve the cache-coherence problem [2]:

1. *Shared cache.* No private processor caches are implemented; the shared cache is associated with the main memory. The processors are interconnected to the shared cache by a communication network. This method violates the principle of closeness of CPU to the cache and may increase the cache access time, degrading the overall performance. The I/O must be serviced through the shared cache to avoid I/O-induced incoherence.

2. *Noncachable shared writable data.* Only instructions and non-shared or non-writable data are allowed to be stored in caches. Such items are called *cachable.* Shared writable data are *noncachable.* The data must be *tagged* accordingly by the compiler and the hardware must adhere to this tagging. The tags are attached to each page of information, and also stored in the CPU *Translation Buffer* (TB). This method introduces an extra overhead (tagging), which may degrade performance and it does not solve the I/O-induced problem. It also causes an extra burden on the user to declare the type of data, that is, cachable or not.

3. *Cache flush.* Shared writable data in a *critical section* (see Chapter 3) can be cached. If a processor works on a critical section in its cache, the critical section is invalidated after the processor completes the execution and modified data have been *written-through* to the main memory. The critical section is flushed from the cache in which it has been worked on. In systems adopting a write-back policy, the design implementing this method will be much more complex. The extra cache flushing tends to degrade performance. The method does not solve the I/O-induced problem.

4. *Centralized global table.* The status of memory blocks is stored in a central global table, residing in the shared main memory. A block can be tagged as *Read Only* (RO) or *Read and Write* (RW). Only one processor cache can have a copy of a block tagged as RW. Other processor caches can have copies of the same block, tagged as RO. This method is effective in keeping cache coherence and it also solves the process migration and the I/O-induced problems. On the other hand, global table access may cause bottlenecks and increase memory latency. This method has been implemented in the IBM 308x systems.

5. *Snoopy cache controller.* A *Block Status Table* is distributed among the processors of the system. The consistency between caches is maintained by a *bus-watching* mechanism, which implements a cache-coherence protocol on the bus. The "snoopy" controller watches for store signals. If a store is made to a cache location also cached in remote caches, then the copies of the block in remote caches are either invalidated or updated. Naturally, the method is implementable in bus-oriented systems. It was used in the Berkeley SPUR and in the Xerox Dragon systems.

Particular care has to be taken in systems implementing methods (4) or (5) in the design of the application of synchronization primitives such as uninterruptible and indivisible read-write-modify memory cycles (see Chapter 3). If two processors are trying to test the same semaphore, it may cause its "bouncing" between the two caches. The design should preclude such a case and permit the transfer of the semaphore into one cache only, until the processor, using the appropriate critical section, has completed its execution.

When a number of processes attempt to access the same memory module through a network, a degradation of performance will result. A concentration of references to a single resource (for instance, a semaphore within a memory module) creates what is called a *hot spot* in the system [6]. The congestion created towards the contested resource increases memory latency not only in that direction; it tends to degrade *all* network traffic. This effect is called *tree saturation*. An effective method which provides a solution to the hot spot problem is *message combining*. It works by detecting the occurrence of memory request messages directed at identical memory locations as they pass through each switch node of the communication network. Such messages are *combined* at the switch node into a *single message*. The fact that the combination took place is recorded in a *wait buffer* in each switch node. When the reply to a combined message reaches a node where it was combined, multiple replies are generated to satisfy the multiple individual requests [6]. The above method of message combining was implemented in the NYU Ultracomputer [3]. A similar approach has been adopted in the experimental IBM RP3 system [7]. The hardware implementation of the message combining method causes significant additional expenses. On the other hand, it requires no additional programming overhead. The additional cost of a hardware-based combining network may be outweighed by its potential advantages, particularly notable for large scale multiprocessor systems. A purely software implementation of the message combining method has also been proposed [8]. A careful hardware-software trade-off analysis should be carried out by the designer in this case.

The design problems, discussed above, are strongly connected with the hardware structure of the multiprocessor system. The software design of a multiprocessor presents no less of a problem (see Chapters 3 and 4). The overall design of a multiprocessor should include an efficient operating system capable of supporting all of the tasks inherent in multiprocessing. Such elements would include:

- process;
- processor;
- multimodule and multi-I/O interface management;
- scheduling;
- synchronization;
- communication; and
- other tasks as described in this and previous chapters.

It should support parallelizing compilers for high-level languages. A detailed example of a multiprocessor (the Alliant) featuring, in detail, both hardware and software aspects is presented in Chapter 7.

References 1. D. D. Gajski, J. K. Peir, "Essential Issues in Multiprocessor Systems," *IEEE Computer*, Vol. 18, No. 6, pp. 9–27, June 1985.

2. M. Dubois, C. Scheurich, F. A. Briggs, "Synchronization, Coherence, and Event Ordering in Multiprocessors," *IEEE Computer*, Vol. 21, No. 2, pp. 9–12, Feb. 1988.

3. A. Gottlieb, et al., "The NYU Ultracomputer-Designing on MIMD Shared Memory Parallel Computer," *IEEE Trans. on Computers*, Vol. C-32, No. 2, pp. 175–189, Feb. 1983.

4. R. Rettberg, R. Thomas, "Contention is no Obstacle to Shared-Memory Multiprocessing," *Comm. ACM*, Vol. 29, No. 12, pp. 1202–1212, Dec. 1986.

5. L. M. Censier, P. Feautrier, "A New Solution to Coherence Problems in Multicache Systems," *IEEE Trans. on Computers*, Vol. C-27, No. 12, pp. 1112–1118, Feb. 1978.

6. G. V. Pfister, V. A. Norton, "Hot Spot Contention and Combining in Multistage Interconnection Networks," *IEEE Trans. on Computers*, Vol. C-34, No. 10, pp. 943–948, Oct. 1985.

7. G. V. Pfister et al., "The IBM Research Parallel Processor Prototype (RP3): Introduction and Architecture," *Proc. 1985 Int. Conf. on Parallel Processing*, pp. 764–771, St. Charles, IL, August, 1985.

8. P. C. Yew, N. F. Tzeng, D. H. Lawrie, "Distributing Hot-Spot Addressing in Large-Scale Multiprocessors," *IEEE Trans. on Computers*, Vol. C-36, No. 4, pp. 388–395, April 1987.

CHAPTER 6

Evaluation of Multiprocessor Performance

Multiprocessors are very complex systems, containing multiple processors, memory modules, I/O interface units, and interconnection networks. Therefore, the evaluation of multiprocessor performance is quite complicated as well. The fact that the same system may perform in a different way for different types of problems, renders the evaluation to be even more difficult. Different problems have different possibilities for parallelization. Some problems can not be parallelized at all. Let us first define two measures for multiprocessor performance [1]. Assume that we have a multiprocessor consisting of n processors. Assume further that we have a program that can be subdivided into processes that can run concurrently on the n processors. Denote the total execution time of the program on the n-processor by $T(n)$. The time it would take to run the same program on a uniprocessor is $T(1)$. We can now define the speedup, S, of a multiprocessor as the ratio of the total uniprocessor execution time and the n-processor execution time of the same program:

$$S = T(1)/T(n)$$

In an ideal situation, when the program can be partitioned into exactly n processes of equal run time (and assuming all n-processors are identical) and with zero overhead (see Chapter 2) we should have $S = n$. In practice, the vast majority of programs can not be partitioned in the above way and there is always some overhead. There is usually a fraction f of all the operations of the program that must be performed sequentially and that can not be parallelized. Therefore, in practice, the speedup S is usually lower than the number of processors n.

For some programs the fraction of sequentially executed instructions, f, is considerable. In this case some of the processors may be idle some of the time. We define the *efficiency* or the *utilization* of a multiprocessor, E, as the ratio of the speedup and the number of processors n.

$$E = S/n = T(1)/[nT(n)]$$

In an ideal case, if we could have $S = n$, the efficiency would be $E = n/n = 1.00$, or: 100%. Since in practice $S < n$, we have $E < 1$. The design and the operation management of a multiprocessor should strive to achieve a value of E as close to unity as possible. A good way to achieve a high value of system utilization is to schedule different programs on different available processors, as it is done in the Alliant, for instance (see Chapter 7).

It has been argued by Amdahl that the following speedup limitation inequality is in effect:

$$S \leq 1/[f + (1 - f)/n] = n/[1 + (n - 1)f]$$

In limit cases, when the program is completely parallelizable and no part of it must be executed sequentially, that is, $f = 0$, we have: $S \leq n$ (or $S = n$ in an ideal case), and if the program is completely sequential, $f = 1$, we have $S \leq 1$; no speedup. In order to maintain 50% efficiency, $E = 0.5$, we need a speedup of $S = En = 0.5n$. Using this in Amdahl's inequality we obtain:

$$n/2 \leq 1/[f + (1 - f)/n]$$

or,

$$nf + 1 - f \leq 2$$

and:

$$f \leq 1/(n - 1)$$

To maintain an efficiency of E, we need:

$$f \leq (1 - E)/[E(n - 1)]$$

In other words, in order to maintain a constant efficiency, the fraction of the computation devoted to sequential processing, f, must be proportional to the inverse of the number of processors n [3].

A much practiced approach to evaluate and compare different multiprocessors is to run a large number of benchmark programs on them and note the differences in total execution time, memory use, and other factors of interest. Other approaches involve queueing models, statistical analysis and simulation [4]. All of these approaches require the dedication of considerable computing time and software effort, and are outside the scope of this discussion. A simple, approximate, fast, preliminary evaluation approach of the performance capability of multiprocessors is discussed in the following [5]. The method uses the manufacturer's specifications and does not require any software effort or computing time.

The performance of a multiprocessor system depends not only on the raw computing power, expressed in *Millions of Instructions Per Second* (MIPS), *Millions of Floating point Operations Per Second* (MFLOPS), the number of processors, and other parameters. The basic communications parameters, such as the nature of the communication network (bus, n-cube, and switch), data bus width, and bus bandwidth (usually expressed in MBytes/sec) will certainly influence the communication overhead, expressed by the C parameter (see Chapter 2). The computing power parameters will influence directly the processing effort capability, expressed by R [6]. The R parameter is actually defined in Stone [6] as the length of a run-time quantum and C and as the length of the communications overhead produced by that quantum. The R is used here in a somewhat different sense. All of the parameters mentioned above, and many others, will have an influence on the R/C ratio, which we would like to increase.

However, the R/C ratio does not depend only on the basic quantitative parameters of the computing system. It will strongly depend on the nature of the program as run on the system along with the basic software available (such as OS or compilers). There may be a problem lending itself to a disjoint parallelization, where separate tasks of the program simultaneously run on separate processors during most of the run time, without a need to communicate intermediate results between the processors. In a case like this, the communication facilities will be used at a minimal level and C will be small. On the other hand, there may be a problem requiring frequent transmission of information between the processors tending to increase C.

A highly sophisticated OS (see Chapter 4) will be capable of efficient automatic parallelization of a program, scheduling of tasks between the processors, exchanging messages between them and other tasks required in a multiprocessor. The quality of the OS, combined with the nature of a program (some programs can not be efficiently parallelized regardless of the quality of the OS), will certainly influence the value of the R/C ratio.

The above factors do not lend themselves to a direct quantitative evaluation. Only a partial evaluation will be presented, using a set of some basic parameters of the system, independent of the nature of the program and the available system software. The results of such a partial evaluation will not be conclusive, but they will be indicative of the performance potential of the system as compared to other systems in the same class.

The following parameters are proportional to the computing effort capability R:

n = number of processors.
m = performance of each processor in MIPS.
f = floating point performance of each processor in MFLOPS.
w = word length of the processor in units of 32 bits. That is, word length = 32w.

For a 32-bit system, w = 1. For a 16-bit system, w = ½. The R parameter is proportional to the product (nmfw). The following parameters are inversely proportional to the communication overhead parameter C:

b = data bus width index in units of 32 lines, such that the data bus width = 32b.
i = interconnection index, defined so that each processor is directly interconnected to p(i − 1) other processors, rounded to the lower integer. For a single-bus interconnection, i = 1. For a p-cube system, where each processor is directly connected to p other processors, i = 2.
d = bus bandwidth in MByte/sec.

The C parameter is proportional to the inverse of the product of the above parameters, 1/(bid).

The R/C ratio is, therefore, proportional to the product (nmfwbid). The dimensionality of the above product may seem bizarre, however we can always multiply it by a coefficient of unity value and an inverse dimensionality, rendering the result dimensionless, but of the same value. This multiplication has no influence on the subsequent development.

Let us take as an example two multiprocessor systems with the following parameters:

Parameter		System 1		System 2	
n	(processors)	8		16	
m	(MIPS)	16		16	
f	(MFLOPS)	8		16	
w		1	(32-bits)	2	(64-bits)
b		4	(4*32 bits)	1	(32 bits)
i		1	(bus)	1	(bus)
d	(MBytes/sec)	32		32	
Pr = nmfwbid		131,072		262,144	

The product Pr, proportional to R/C, is twice as large for system 2 as compared to system 1. It indicates that system 2 has a good chance to perform more efficiently for many problems than system 1. As argued before, this conclusion is only indicative and by no means conclusive. The Pr index turns out to be rather large. If more parameters are added to the consideration it will only increase and become inconvenient to handle. It is, therefore, convenient to introduce a LOGARITHMIC INDEX. It will be agreed that logx will represent the logarithm of x on basis 2. The logarithmic index is defined as:

$$L = logPr = log(nmfwbid) =$$

$$= logn + logm + logf + logw + logb + logi + logd$$

Introducing the notation:

$N = logn \quad M = logm; \quad F = logf; \quad W = logw;$
$B = logb; \quad I = logi; \quad D = logd;$

we have:

$$L = N + M + F + W + B + I + D$$

In general, if we have a set of parameters xi, i = 1, . . , k, and Xi = logxi, i = 1, . . . , k, then

$$Pr = \prod_{i=1}^{k} xi$$

and

$$L = \sum_{i=1}^{k} Xi$$

Continuing the previous example we now have:

Logarithmic Index	System 1	System 2
N	3	4
M	4	4
F	3	4
W	0	1
B	2	0
I	0	0
D	5	5
L	17	18

The L values are much more convenient to handle.

The above parameters are hardware-based. However, we can easily add software considerations when using the approach of logarithmic indices.

We can add parameters directly to the logarithmic scale. For instance, we can agree that if system 2 has a parallelizing OS, it will be assigned an extra logarithmic index O = 1. If system 1 does not have one, then O = 0. If the OS of system 2 has special provisions for the efficient handling of real-time operations, an extra index R = 1 can be assigned to it. If system 1 does not have this capability, R = 0. Now, for system 1, L is still 17, while for system 2, L = 20. Taking into account that we have a logarithmic scale, we have a very strong indication that system 2 should be selected for a real-time multiprocessor implementation (see Chapter 14).

Not all of the logarithmic indices may be of the same importance for a particular application. Different weights can be assigned:

$$LW = \sum_{i=1}^{k} W_i X_i$$

For normalization we can assume: $W_1 + W_2 \ldots + W_k = 1$.

Example: The method of logarithmic indices is applied to a selected set of three representative commercial multiprocessors: Alliant FX/80 (see Chapter 7), ELXSI System 6400 (using the 6460 CPU) (see Chapter 8), and Intel iPSC/2 (see Chapter 9). The basic data are:

Parameter	Alliant		ELXSI		iPSC/2
n (processors)	8		12		128
m (MIPS/CPU)	4		25		4
f (MFLOPS/CPU)	23.6		10		1
w	1	(32-bit)	2	(64-bit)	1
b	3		2		1
i	1	(bus)	1	(bus)	2
d (MBytes/sec)	188		320		32

The corresponding logarithmic indices:

Index	Alliant	ELXSI	iPSC/2
N	3	3.5	7
M	2	4.6	2
F	4.6	3.3	0
W	0	1	0
B	1.5	1	0
I	0	0	1
D	7.5	8.3	5
L	18.6	21.7	15

The above tabulation strongly favors the ELXSI system, however, if relative weighting is introduced, a different result may be obtained. Although the above evaluation is only partial, the resulting *Logarithmic Index* (L) for each system considered, yields a fairly indicative representation of the system's potential performance capability. The above example is intended to illustrate the application of the method of logarithmic indices and should not be regarded as a conclusive evaluation of the above systems.

References
1. J. P. Hayes, *Computer Organization and Architecture, 2nd. ed.*, McGraw-Hill, NY, 1988, Chapter 7.

2. G. Amdahl, "Validity of the Single Processor Approach to Achieving Large Scale Computing Capabilities, "*Proc. AFIPS Conference*, Vol. 30, pp. 483–485, Thompson Books, Washington, D.C. 1967.

3. M. J. Quinn, *Designing Efficient Algorithms for Parallel Computers*, McGraw-Hill, NY, 1987.

4. H. S. Stone, ed., *Introduction to Computer Architecture, 2nd. ed.*, Science Research Associates, Chicago, IL, 1980.

5. D. Tabak, "Logarithmic Indices for Multiprocessor Evaluation," *Computer Architecture News*, Vol. 16, No. 1, pp. 85–90, March 1988.

6. H. S. Stone, *High-performance Computer Architecture*, Addison-Wesley, Reading, MA, 1987, Chapter 6.

PART TWO

EXAMPLES OF COMMERCIAL MULTIPROCESSORS

CHAPTER 7

Detailed Example—The Alliant System

7.1 Introductory Comments

Commercial multiprocessing made its appearance in the third generation of computer development [1]. The starting point of the third generation was the mid-1960s with the birth of the IBM 360 system, which was later followed by IBM 370, 308x, 3090 and others. In parallel with the above, the CDC 6600 and the CYBER family was developed. The CDC CYBER 70/74, IBM 370/168MP and IBM 3081 were dual processors, the IBM 3084 had four processors [2]. The IBM 3090 can be configured for up to six processors [3]. The Cray X-MP is a dual processor and Cray 2 had four processors [2]. All of the above are powerful mainframe computers, some of which (Cray, for instance) are labeled as *supercomputers*.

The development of multiprocessing ideas started even before the announcement of the third generation systems. We can find a record of definite multiprocessing ideas in the IBM Stretch Project (1956–1961), as documented by Buchholtz [4], Ch. 13:

. . . nonlocal concurrency, provides for simultaneous execution of instructions which need not be neighbors in an instruction stream but which may belong to entirely separate and unrelated programs. A computer system, in order to exhibit nonlocal concurrency, must possess a number of connected *facilities*, each capable of operating simultaneously (and except for memory references, independently) on programs that need not be related to one another. A facility may be an I/O unit, an external storage unit, an arithmetic unit, a logic unit, or some assemblage of these units. In an extreme case each facility is a complete computer itself. . . . programs can be subdivided into . . . tasks. At any instant the tasks being executed simultaneously may belong all to one program or to different programs.

The above ideas can certainly be considered as a precursor to the modern development of multiprocessor systems. A detailed exposition of any of the multiprocessors mentioned above (such as Cray 2 or IBM 3090) could serve as an excellent example. However, beginning in the 1980s, a new trend of commercial multiprocessing has emerged. Due to the development of VLSI technology, it became possible to manufacture high-performance and relatively low-cost multiprocessors. Some of the individual processors in the above multiprocessors are actually microprocessor chips, such as Motorola MC68020, National NS32332, or Intel 80386. Some of these new multiprocessors can even be called *multimicroprocessors*.

The low cost of the new multiprocessors made them accessible to a much wider public of users. It is for this reason that the example systems in this chapter and in Chapters 8 through 11 have been selected. In particular, the Alliant system has been chosen to be presented in a detailed example. There are several reasons for this choice:

1. Alliant has a unique multibus structure (see Chapter 2); two system buses (CPU-memory), and one concurrency bus between the processors [5].

2. The Alliant implements an additional crossbar interconnection network between the processors and the cache modules (again, a unique feature).

3. It has two types of processors:

   (a) Custom made for concurrent processing of processes belonging to the same or different programs; and

   (b) Off-the-shelf (MC68020) for interactive processing, running the OS and other utility programs.

4. It has automatically partitioning HLL compiler the FX/FORTRAN, capable of allocating instances of a DO-loop among the processors for different index values of the loop.

5. It has become significantly wide spread both on national and international markets.

It would certainly be of interest to provide a detailed description on many systems. However, this would make our text unnecessarily too bulky. There are many features which appear in several systems and repetitions should be avoided. It was, therefore, decided to present a detailed example of a single system, the Alliant, for the reasons listed above. This will be done in the subsequent sections of this chapter.

Other systems will be surveyed, in less detail, in the subsequent chapters. Although the discussion of other systems will be less detailed, it will be sufficient to give the reader a comprehensive idea about the main properties of these systems, their architecture, structure and software capabilities.

7.2 Alliant System Structure

A general diagram of the full configuration of the Alliant FX system is shown in Figure 7.1 [5]. It consists of the following main subsystems:

- *Computational Elements* (CE), a total of eight. The CE is the primary processor intended for parallel, concurrent operation. It is the main building block of the system.

- *Interactive Processors* (IP), a total of 12. The IP is intended for interactive user processing, the Operating System (OS), I/O, and utility programs.

- *Computational Processor Cache* (CP Cache), two units of 256 KByte each.

- *Interactive Processor Cache* (IP Cache), four units of 32 KBytes each.

- *Main Memory*, eight modules of 32 MBytes (ECC) for a total fo 256 MBytes, realized by one Mbit dynamic RAMs, four-way interleaved (for each module).

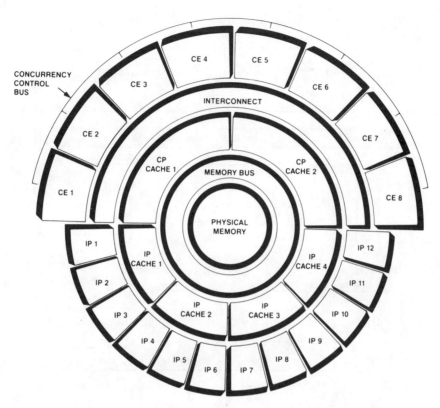

FIGURE 7.1. The Alliant system (courtesy of Alliant Computer Sys. Corp.).

- *Crossbar Interconnect Network* between the CEs and the CP Cache, 376 MBytes/sec.
- *Memory Bus*, 2∗72bits dual bus, 188 MBytes/sec bandwidth.
- *Concurrency Control Bus*, a special 40-line interconnection for parallel processing information transmission between the CEs.

The above is the maximal configuration of the FX/8 model. Alternative configurations, with less components of each type, are available, such as FX/4 with up to 4CEs or a single CE FX/1.

The CE is a microprogrammed, pipelined processor with integrated floating point and vector instruction sets. It is an Alliant proprietary processor, realized by 64-bit CMOS gate arrays. Its architecture constitutes an extended version of that of the Motorola MC68020 [6]. A block diagram of the CE is shown in Figure 7.2.

The CE is organized into four main functional units:

1. *Instruction unit* consists of a five-stage pipeline that allows instructions to be executed every machine cycle provided no resource or data conflicts exist. The instruction unit includes the following subunits:

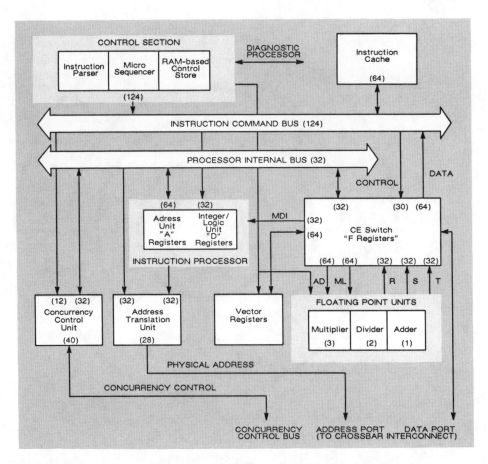

FIGURE 7.2. Computational element (CE) block diagram.

(a) *Instruction Cache* consists of 16 KBytes and 85 nsec RAM addressed on each CE with logical addresses. In case of a miss, the instruction cache controller initiates a load.

(b) *Control Section* consists of:
   (i) *Instruction Parser* which receives opcodes from the data path and decodes them to generate control store microaddresses. The parser also stores the instruction fields of the opcodes that are in various stages of execution, checks for dependencies between instructions, and prevents a new instruction from starting when dependencies exist. It includes a branch prediction unit that anticipates the most likely flow of program control and prefetches instructions.

   (ii) *Microsequencer* contains registers for delaying the execution of certain fields of a microword, logic for decoding delayed fields, and sequencing logic for controlling microtraps and unaligned memory references.

   (iii) *Control Store* is RAM-based and contains the control microcode of the CE.

(c) *Instruction Processor* consists of:

(i) *Address Unit* which is implemented as a pair of 8000-gate CMOS gate arrays and consists of two identical 16-bit slices. It contains the instruction buffer, the address data path, and the address unit of control logic. The instruction buffer receives the output of the instruction caches, latches it, and rotates 16-bit words to align the opcode, immediate data, immediate addresses, and displacements. The address data path contains eight address (A) Registers, the Program Counter (PC), a 32-bit adder, a variable shifter, multiplexors, and temporary registers for implementing various addressing modes. The address unit control logic generates address data path controls from opcodes.

(ii) *Integer/Logic Unit* is implemented as an 8000-gate CMOS gate array. The unit's 32-bit data path contains eight data (D) registers, four integer temporaries, an ALU, a full barrel shifter, and a programmable two-cycle microinstruction delay shift register to aid in macroinstruction pipelining.

(d) *Address Translation Unit* (ATU) performs logical-to-physical address translation and contains the logical address register, which is loaded from the address unit. The ATU includes a translation cache, which stores recently used address translations and access checking hardware.

2. *Floating Point and Vector Unit* which is implemented in custom NMOS VLSI and 8000-gate CMOS gate arrays. The following operational units are included:

| | | | *170 nsec cycles* | |
Unit	Quantity	Bits	Scalar	Vector
Floating Point Add/Sub/Convert	1	32	2	1
		64	3	1
Floating Point Multiplication	2	32	2	1
		64	3	1
Floating Point Division	2	32	9	4
		64	16	7.5
Integer Multiplication	1	32	4	1

The following Floating Point and Vector Registers are included:

Register name	Quantity	Length	Width
Floating Point Data	8	1	64
Floating Point States	1	1	32
Floating Point Control	1	1	32
Vector Data	8	32	64
Vector Length	1	1	32
Vector Increment	1	1	32
Vector Mask	1	1	32

Each of the 64-bit floating point data registers holds a 32-bit or 64-bit precision floating point number.

3. *Concurrency Control Unit (CCU)* which connects the CEs of the computational complex through an independent 40-bit Concurrency Control Bus. Implemented as an 8000-gate CMOS array. The CCU interfaces with the Instruction Unit of a CE and up to seven other CCUs to transparently control up to eight CEs running concurrently (see Figure 7.3). Since *all parallel processing* is *controlled* at *execution time*, there is no compile-time dependency on the size of the system. Once programs are compiled to run concurrently, they will execute on a complex of from one to eight CEs. This allows for field ungradable performance by simply adding CEs with no reprogramming, recompiling, or relinking.

4. *CE switch* which is an internal interconnection between the units of the CE.

The IP is an industry-standard Multibus card containing a Motorola MC 68020 microprocessor, two MBytes of local memory and console and remote diagnostic serial ports. The IP is also available as an MC68020-based VME card with four MBytes local memory. It interfaces with the IP Cache, which provides access to the main memory, and to a Multibus (IEEE 796 compatible), which provides access to I/O devices. Virtual address space for users is two GBytes. A *Direct Memory Access* (DMA) channel operating through the I/O map, enables multibus devices to perform DMA anywhere within the physical address space. The *System IP* is identical to other IPs except that it connects to the system console and remote diagnostic port.

The *System IP* bootstraps the system by executing diagnostic software, controlling the system diagnostic bus, and handling other system housekeeping tasks. A local program-controlled clock allows the System IP to function as a totally self-contained processor so that it can diagnose the rest of the system.

FIGURE 7.3. CCU interconnections (courtesy of Alliant Computer Sys. Corp.).

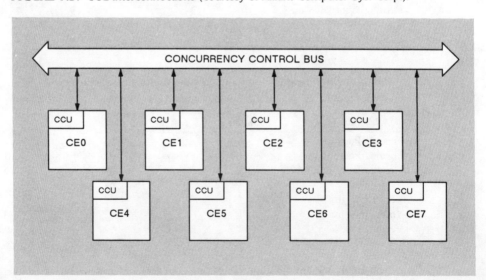

A single *CP Cache* module can serve as a two-way interleaved, 256 KByte, 85nsec access cache for up to four CEs. Two such modules provide a four-way interleaved 512 KByte cache with a maximum bandwidth of 376 MBytes/sec. Each module is subdivided into two 128 KBytes banks or quadrants (see Figure 7.4). The CP Cache is designed to support multiple cache accesses in parallel. Up to three cache accesses can be pending in each of the four cache quadrants, for a total of up to 12 accesses pending in the entire cache. The CP Cache implements a *write-back* policy of main memory update. This design realizes the shared cache principle (see Chapter 5) to maintain cache coherence. In addition, a bus-watching hardware-based mechanism, transparent to the user, is implemented. An example is illustrated in Figure 7.5.

Cache A has just requested a copy of a block from main memory. However, a copy of this block has been modified and is currently residing in cache B. Cache B monitors the memory address bus and detects that a request is being made for a copy of a block that it has modified. Cache B intercepts the memory read operation initialized by cache A. It sends a copy of its modified block to cache A and to main memory.

The *IP Cache* is field expandable from one to four 32 KBytes, 85nsec, modules for a maximum of 128 KBytes. Each module supports up to three IPs. A cache module that wants to write any given block must first obtain a "unique" copy of the block. Thus, while any module may have a copy of a block, only one can have a writable copy. In the previous coherency example, if cache A has requested a unique (or writable) copy of the block, then cache B will automatically invalidate its copy of the block. (See the Centralized Global Table cache coherence approach in Chapter 5).

Each IP Cache supports three external ports of 11.76 MByte/sec, 16 bit for IPs. The IP Cache I/O bandwidth:

FIGURE 7.4. CE, cache, and memory bus interconnections (courtesy of Alliant Computer Sys. Corp.).

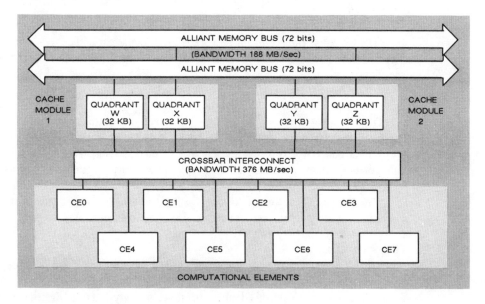

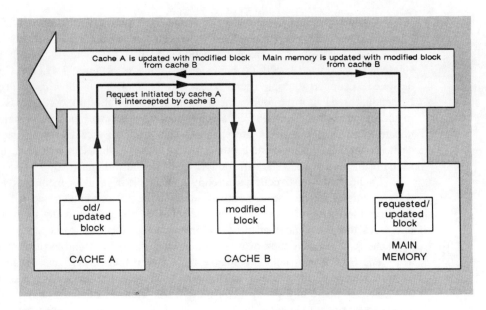

FIGURE 7.5. Cache coherency handling (courtesy of Alliant Computer Sys. Corp.).

Interface Type	Continuous Bandwidth (MBytes/sec)
Memory bus to IP cache	94.10
Cache to 16-bit port	11.70
IP cache to IPs	3.92
IP to multibus	1.96

The *Crossbar Interconnect Network* is a 4 × 8 address and data switch implemented in twenty-four 2600-gate arrays. It provides a sustained bandwidth of 376 MBytes/sec (see Figure 7.4).

The *Aliant Memory Bus* is a high-speed, synchronous memory access bus that consists of two 72-bit wide bidirectional data paths, a 28-bit address bus, and a control bus. Data is always transferred as four eight-byte words (a "cache block"), with the first word transferred on data bus A. Thereafter, the data alternates between data bus A and data bus B for four cycles. Of the 72 bits of data, 64 are for actual data and eight for error detection. The memory bus allows up to eight block accesses to be in progress at any one time.

The Alliant FX/1 consists of one CE, up to two IPs, 64 MBytes of main memory and a 32 KByte system cache. There is also a more recent FX/4 system, consisting of up to four CEs, six IPs, 128 MBytes of main memory, 256 KBytes CE cache and 64 KBytes IP cache.

The Alliant CE has undergone further development and there is an upgraded processor *Advanced Computational Element* (ACE). The ACE has the same architecture as the CE, however its speed is double, due to technology and organization enhancements.

It can sustain 23.6 MFLOPS peak performance. The ACE is the processor for the following systems (the FX/8 data are repeated for comparison):

	FX/80		FX/40		FX/8	
ACE	8		4			
CE					8	
IP (68020-based)	12		9		12	
Main memory	256	MB	160	MB	256	MB
CP Cache	512	KB	256	KB	512	KB
IP Cache	128	KB	96	KB	128	KB

Valid configurations for the FX/40 are as follows:

Memory Total (MBytes)	IP Total	IP Cache Total (KBytes)
96	9	96
128	6	64
160	3	32

Two FX/80 systems can be clustered to form the FX/82 with 16 ACEs and 24 IPs capable of concurrent operation. The FX/82 can achieve 377.6 peak MFLOPS performance. Its performance is estimated to be seven times that of the four-processor VAX8840.

7.3 Alliant System Architecture

The CE architecture [7] is an extension of the architecture of the Motorola MC68020 [6]. That is, it contains most of the architectural features of the MC68020, plus some additional ones, particular to the Alliant CE proprietary design. The IP uses an actual MC68020 as its CPU. Since the architecture of the MC68020, is well documented, its details will not be repeated here. Only the new Alliant CE features and details which differ from those in the MC68020 will be discussed here.

The CE has about 250 different instructions. Considering the fact that most of the instructions can be applied to a number of data types (bytes, words, and longwords), the full complement of instructions exceeds 700. The CE instructions are subdivided into four basic categories:

1. *Base* consisting of most of the MC68020 instructions.
2. *Floating Point* implementing arithmetic, transcedental, test, and move operations on floating point data.
3. *Vector* implementing integer and floating point operations on up to 32 data elements at a time.
4. *Concurrency* implementing the parallel execution of instructions by multiple processors.

Categories (2) through (4) are new and were not available with the MC68020. Since floating point operations are integrated within the CE, there is no separate floating point coprocessor as in the MC68000 family. Thus, all MC68020 coprocessor instructions (with the "cp" prefix) are not implemented by the CE.

The instruction formats and the integer data types are the same as in the MC68020. In fact, the CE recognizes all of the data types of the MC68020. The CE has two additional data types:

(a) *Floating Point Data*. According to IEEE standard:

> Single precision, 32 bits: 23 mantissa, 8 exponent, 1 sign
> Double precision, 64 bits: 52 mantissa, 11 exponent, 1 sign

(b) *Vector Data*. A *vector* consists of up to 32 *elements*, which can be integer or floating point. The *number of elements* is called the *vector length*. The elements can be *adjacent* or can be separated by a constant *stride* in their storage location. The stride is called the vector *increment* and is *measured in multiples of the element size*. A vector with adjacent elements has a vector increment of one. A vector of identical elements drawn from the same memory location has an increment of zero. A vector whose elements run from high memory to low memory has a negative increment.

The CE contains the same CPU general reigsters as the MC68020 and some new ones. In particular, it has the eight Data Registers, (d0-d7), and the eight Address Registers (a0-a7) as in MC68020 (D0-D7, A0-A7). The a7 register is used as a *Stack Pointer* (SP) in the same way as the A7 in MC68020. The new general registers are:

1. *Floating Point Registers* (8, 64-bit, denoted fp0-fp7). The entire floating point register is affected even for single precision (32-bit) operations.
2. *Vector Registers* (8 denoted v0-v7). Each vector register consists of 32 elements, 64-bits each (2048 bits total), that is, a 32×64 structure. The elements are numbered consecutively, 0 to 31.

The control registers, *Program Counter* (PC), *Stack Pointer* (SP, a7) and the 16-bit *Status Register*, are implemented in the same way as in MC68020. There is however a slight difference in the use of the Status Register (see Figure 7.6). Three bits (11, 7, 6) not implemented in the MC68020, are now used, as shown in Figure 7.6. Bit 5 remains unimplemented.

There are two control registers for floating point operations:

1. *Floating Point Status Register* (FPSR)—a 32-bit register that contains the floating point condition codes.
2. *Floating Point Control Register* (FPCR)—a 32-bit register that contains the control encoding for floating point operation.

The floating point condition flags are:

• *Negative*—set if the result of the comparison is a non-zero negative number of infinity.
• *Zero*—set if the result of the comparison is zero.
• *Not a number*—set if the result of the comparison cannot be represented mathematically.

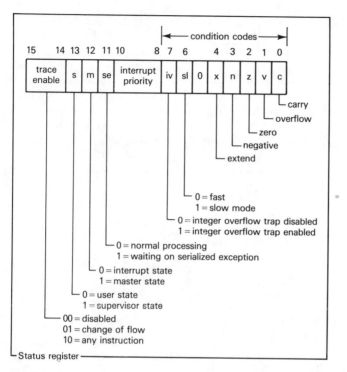

FIGURE 7.6. The status register (courtesy of Alliant Computer Sys. Corp.).

Data registers d4, d5 and d6 serve as control registers for vector operations. They must be loaded, prior to using a vector instruction, with the following values:

d4 (can be addressed as v1) holds the vector *length*.

d5 (or:vi) holds the vector *increment* (stride from the beginning of one vector element in memory to the next element). The stride is a multiple of the element size.

d6 (or:vm) holds the vector *mask*. For any vm bit set, the corresponding vector element will be processed.

The internal processor registers (to be used by the system only) SFC, DFC, USP, MSP, ISP, VBR are treated as in the MC68020.

The CE addressing modes are the same as in the MC68020. The binary machine code is identical, however the assembly language notation is different in the CE.

Most of the original MC68020 instructions appear also in the CE, except that instructions BKPT, CALLM, CAS, CAS2, all cp prefixed, RTM are not supported by the Alliant CE. The MC68020 RESET instruction is treated as a "no operation" by the CE. The CE has sets of floating point, vector and concurrency instructions, not supported by the MC68020.

Most of the CE exception vectors are the same as in the MC68020, with the following differences:

Exception Number	MC68020	Alliant CE
0	reset	unassigned
1	reset	unassigned
2	bus error	memory management
7	cctrapcc, trapcc, trapv	trapcc, trapv
12	unassigned	reserved STE or PTE
13	coprocessor protocol	unassigned
16	unassigned	integer overflow
17	unassigned	machine check
25	level 1 interrupt	unassigned
26	level 2 interrupt	unassigned
27	level 3 interrupt	unassigned
28	level 4 interrupt	unassigned
30	level 6 interrupt	unassigned
48	unassigned	floating point exception,

where
PTE = Page table entry
STE = Segment table entry

associated with the memory management.

The *memory management* mechanism of the CE is different from that of the MC68020. As in the MC68020, the CE supports four *addressing spaces* in the Virtual Address Space:

• User Data

• User Program;

• Supervisor Data; and

• Supervisor Program.

Unlike the MC68020, each CE addressing space contains 1024 *segments*, numbered 0 through 1023. Each segment contains 1024 *pages*, numbered 0 through 1023. Each page contains 4096 bytes, numbered 0 through 4095.

The *Physical Memory* consists of addressable bytes numbered consecutively starting at address 0. The highest possible physical address is $2**28-1$. Memory management divides physical memory into a series of *pages* numbered consecutively starting at 0. Each page is 4096 bytes in size, so that page 0 starts at byte 0, page 1 at byte 4096, and so on.

A *Virtual Address* (32 bits) consists of three fields (see Figure 7.7):

1. *Byte* (bits 0–11) identifies a byte within the page.

2. *Page* (bits 12–21) identifies a page within the segment.

3. *Segment* (bits 22–31) identifies a segment in virtual memory.

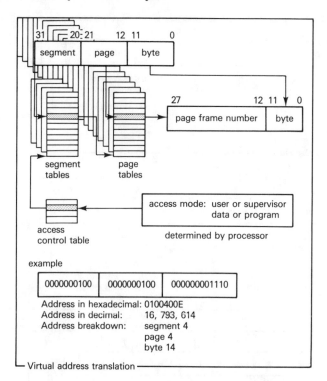

segment page byte

27   12 11 0
page frame number | byte

segment tables   page tables

access control table

access mode: user or supervisor
            data or program

determined by processor

example

| 0000000100 | 0000000100 | 000000001110 |

Address in hexadecimal: 0100400E
Address in decimal: 16, 793, 614
Address breakdown: segment 4
                       page 4
                       byte 14

Virtual address translation

FIGURE 7.7. Virtual address translation (courtesy of Alliant Computer Sys. Corp.).

A *Physical Address* (28 bits) consists of two fields:

1. *Byte,* lowest 12 bits identify a byte within the page.
2. *Page frame number* (pfn), the high order 16 bits identify a page within physical memory.

The low order 12 bits of a virtual address map directly to the low order 12 bits of a physical address. The high order 20 bits of a virtual address (the segment and page numbers) point to a physical page through three tables (see Figure 7.7), which must be supplied by software:

1. *Access Control Table* (ACT)—consists of four *Access Control Table Entries* (ACTEs) (Figures 7.7 and 7.8), which are stored not in memory but in four internal CE registers:

   • SDA—contains the Supervisor Data ACTE.
   • SPA—contains the Supervisor Program ACTE.
   • UDA—contains the User Data ACTE.
   • UPA—contains the User Program ACTE.

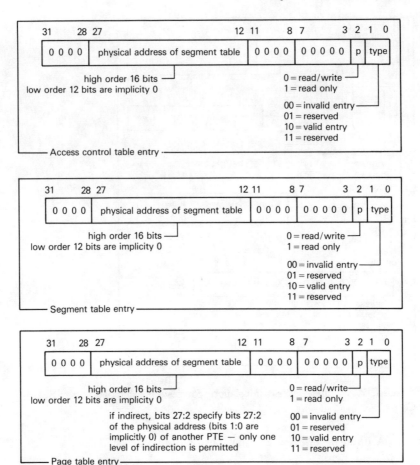

FIGURE 7.8. Translation table entry formats (courtesy of Alliant Computer Sys. Corp.).

Each ACTE points to a segment table for the indicated category of access.

2. *Segment Table* (ST)—consists of up to 1024 four-byte entries. Each valid Segment Table Entry (STE), (Figure 7.8), points to a page table. A segment table must start on a page boundary.

3. *Page Table* (PT)—consists of up to 1,024 four-byte entries. Each valid Page Table Entry (PTE) (Figure 7.8), points to a page in physical memory. A page table must start on a page boundary.

The processor constructs a physical address by determining the page frame number from the tables and high order 20 bits of the virtual address. The 12 low order bits of the virtual address are then concatenated with the page frame number yielding a complete physical memory address.

The processor caches the most recently used PTEs and STEs in an internal buffer as translations are made. The buffer can hold at least 1536 PTEs and 384 STEs. The processor always first attempts to determine the page frame from entries in the translation buffer. If not found, it accesses the tables in memory.

The Alliant *concurrency* instructions [7] permits the concurrent execution of iterations of a loop across multiple processors in a CE complex. The user does not need to know the number of processors in the complex, or whether the program will run in a complex or not. If the program is executed on a CE complex, the loop automatically executes across all available processors. This type of operation is fully supported by the CE hardware, particularly by its synchronization, concurrency control and CCU status registers.

Each CE has eight four-bit *Synchronization Registers* (CS0 through CS7) which can be used to stop execution of a concurrent loop iteration until a previous loop iteration reaches a certain point. The *cawait* (concurrency await synchronization register advance) instruction specifies the point for stopping execution in the current iteration. The *cadvance* (advance synchronization register) instruction must be reached in the previous iteration for execution of the current iteration to resume.

There are eight 32-bit Concurrency Control Registers implicitly manipulated by the concurrency instructions:

1. *cmax* (maximum iteration) contains the maximum iteration count for a concurrent loop in progress.

2. *cnext* (nest outer iteration) contains the low order portion of the number of the next iteration for an outer (not nested) concurrent loop in progress. The upper (33rd) bit is stored in the CCU Status Register.

3. *ccurr* (current iteration) contains the low order portion of the number of the current iteration of a concurrent loop. The upper (33rd) bit is stored in the CCU Status Register.

4. *ccsp* (base-of-cactus stack pointer) holds the address of a stack for storing local variables during concurrent loop execution.

5. *cgsp* (global stack pointer) broadcasts the SP(a7) to other CEs prior to starting a concurrent loop.

6. *cgpc* (global program counter) broadcasts the PC to other CEs prior to starting a concurrent loop.

7. *cgfp* (global frame pointer) broadcasts the frame pointer (a6) to other CEs prior to starting a concurrent loop.

8. *cipc* (idle instruction address) holds the address of the cidle instruction, which is continuously executed by CEs that are not in use (idle).

The *CCU Status Register* (cstat) is a 32-bit register containing information pertaining to the status of a concurrent operation in progress. Among other data, it contains in bits 3–0 the *virtual processor number* (vpn) that uniquely identifies a CE within a CE complex. The vpn has a value in the range 0 through n-1, inclusive, where n is the number of CEs in the complex. Bits 7–4 contain the value of *num* (the largest vpn in the complex). Other bits of the cstat contain various flags related to concurrent operation, such as *nested* (bit 9), which is set for a nested loop, or *detached* (bit 12), which is set if the CE is detached (not within a complex).

Some examples of concurrency instructions are:

* *cstart*—start concurrent loop.
* *cquit*—exit concurrent loop.
* *cidle*—place CE in idle state.
* *cmove to*—load CCU Status Register.
* *cmove from*—store CCU Status Register.
* *crepeat*—branch, if more iterations.

7.4   Alliant OS: The Concentrix

The Concentrix OS [5] is the Alliant implementation of UNIX. It is a general purpose, time-sharing OS for scientific and engineering applications. Concentrix is based on the 4.2 BSD version of the UNIX OS [8,9] and the extended UNIX developed at the University of California at Berkeley. The Concentrix is structured in three layers (see Figure 7.9):

1. The kernel;
2. The shell; and
3. The range of languages and utilities.

The kernel is the machine-dependent core of Concentrix and contains the basic hardware interfaces, process control, and memory management software. Among a variety of features, it supports multiprocessing (both multiprogramming and multitasking), multiple computing resources, demand-paged virtual memory, shared memory, high bandwidth paging/swapping I/O, workstation networks, and real-time applications (see also Chapter 4).

Concentrix maintains queues of ready-to-run jobs for three separate classes of computing resources:

1. Computational complex—a number of CEs in parallel;
2. Detached CEs; and
3. IPs.

Concentrix schedules all three resource classes simultaneously and switches jobs between resource classes to maintain optimum computational throughput.

Under the control of Concentrix, the computational complex can quickly break apart into separate detached CEs. These dynamically detached CEs become available to Concentrix as additional resources. For instance, IP jobs can be offloaded to free CEs. This flexibility allows the Concentrix to keep the utilization factor of the Alliant

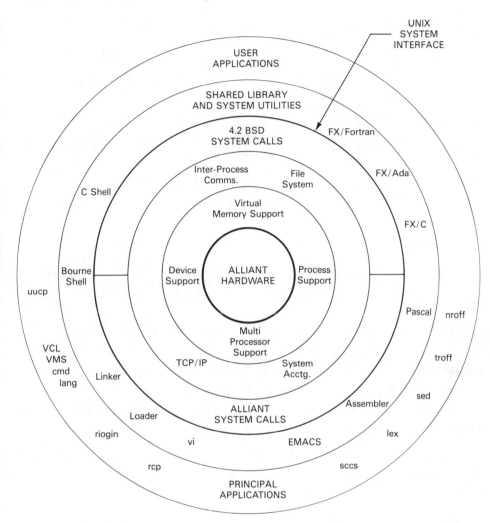

FIGURE 7.9. The concentrix OS (courtesy of Alliant Computer Sys. Corp.).

system at a high level. An example of a possible execution configuration is shown in Figure 7.10. In this case four CEs:CE1-CE4 constitute a computational complex, running job A in a parallel partitioned mode. The rest of the CEs work as detached processors on nine more jobs (B–J). Even then, some jobs can be partitioned for parallel execution on more than one CE:job C runs on CE5, CE6, and CE7 at some time intervals.

Concentrix memory management is demand-paged and supports a physical address space of 256 MBytes and a virtual address space up to two GBytes per process.

To provide support for real-time applications, the Concentrix scheduler supports the assignment of dedicated computing resources to identified user processes. Concentrix has the ability to lock a process into a single-computing resource (computational complex, detached CE, or IP). These processes can use shared memory for interprocess communication. Figure 7.11 illustrates a real-time system that uses all three types of the Alliant computing resources. The shared memory environment allows fast data passing between

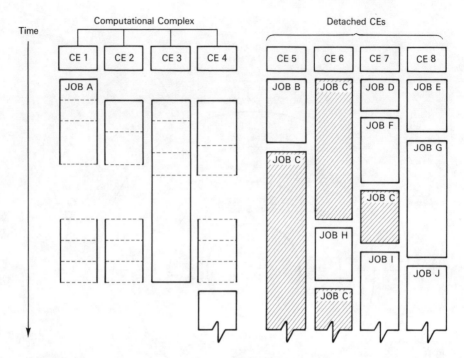

FIGURE 7.10. The concentrix modes of execution (courtesy of Alliant Computer
Sys. Corp.).

processors and avoids context switching and OS kernel services, essentially implementing
a zero-latency real-time system.

The Concentrix Shell is a command language interpreter that is also a powerful
programming language. Typically the shell executes commands by creating processes.
Concentrix implements the C shell of 4.2 BSD UNIX, as well as the AT & T Bourne
Shell [9].

FIGURE 7.11. An example of real-time processing on the FX (courtesy of Alliant
Computer Sys. Corp.).

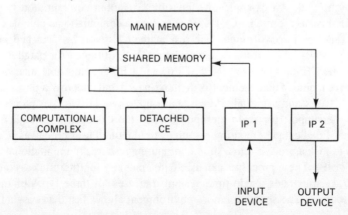

Concentrix includes a group of utilities that provide a highly organized and efficient programming environment. The *Source Code Control System* (SCCS), helps control and account for changes to text files (typically source code and documentation). SCCS maintains an audit trail that includes time and date recording of all changes to a given data base by authorized users.

Make is a program that automates many of the activities of program development and maintenance. Using stored information on inter-file dependencies and command sequences, make updates program files by performing only the necessary operations.

To facilitate program development, Concentrix supports high-level language and assembly language debuggers. The *Source-level Debugger* (dbx) enables program developers to easily explore, display, and modify variables within a running program. As the programmer steps through the program, dbx displays the source code, making it easier to monitor execution and isolate bugs. The *Assembly Language Debugger* (ADB), allows users to examine stack traces, view the contents of registers, and set breakpoints at individual assembly language instructions.

Other Concentrix utilities include document preparation utilities (nroff, troff, sed, and lex) a parser generator, calculator functions, high-level language macro facilities, and pattern manipulation facilities.

The Concentrix system monitor, mon, monitors the utilization of system resources and displays status information in real time. Mon has three modes of operation:

(a) In *family mode*, mon monitors a target process and all of its descendent processes.

(b) In *system mode*, mon monitors all processes in the system.

(c) In *computing resource mode*, mon displays a bar graph showing the state of each installed IP, detached CE, and the computational complex.

Concentrix supports FX/FORTRAN, FX/Ada, FX/C, Pascal, and the Alliant assembler (FX/FORTRAN is discussed in the next section).

FX/Ada's transparent parallel tasking allows a single Ada program to execute in parallel across the CEs and IPs. FX/Ada has been validated by the U.S. Department of Defense.

The FX/C compiler provides automatic parallel and vector processing. The compiler automatically detects the potential for parallel and vector processing in standard C code and generates instructions that use the parallel vector features of the Alliant hardware. Users can also explicitly perform operations that take advantage of the parallel vector architecture. Inline expansion of functions enables the compiler to make further optimizations and increase performance. Users can instruct the compiler to perform inline expansion of functions on already optimized code by inserting pragma directives into the source code or by using compile-time switches and not changing source code. The compiler makes automatic use of the multiple processors to perform multiple simultaneous operations.

Alliant also features the portable, Bell Laboratories-based C compiler. The FX/C compiles about two to three times faster than the portable compiler. The FX/C is compatible with draft ANSI Standard X3J11 for the base C language. It mixes routines and shares data with FORTRAN, Ada and Pascal.

The Pascal compiler is based on the Berkeley UNIX 4.2 compiler for the DEC VAX. It supports the 32-bit CE scalar instruction set and Alliant floating point instructions. LISP and APL for the Alliant are available from third party organizations.

All of the languages, implemented on the Alliant, share a common calling convention. Routines can be written in any of these languages and call each other directly.

The Alliant assembler supports the 32-bit scalar instruction set and Alliant instructions for floating point, vectors, and concurrency.

Concentrix allows Alliant systems to be tightly integrated into networks of engineering workstations providing both compute and file services. Support is provided to interconnect to the Appollo Computer DOMAIN environment and to Sun Microsystems workstations through TCP/IP with full kernel-level support for the *Sun Network File System* (NFS).

Alliant systems offered by Apollo as DSP9000 computational servers can be integrated into a high-speed DOMAIN token-ring network. DOMAIN networks offer users sophisticated remote file sharing capabilities. All network files, no matter where they are located, appear to users as a single file system, and can be transparently accessed without the need of file transfers.

The Sun Network File System provides transparent access and sharing of files in a multi-vector heterogenous environment. File systems, physically mounted on another machine on the network, can be logically mounted in any other file system. A program can then read and write to that remote file without copying the entire file back and forth across the network.

7.5 A Parallelizing Compiler: FX/FORTRAN

The FX/FORTRAN compiler [5, 10] is a highly effective optimizing compiler designed to run on Alliant FX/Series computers. FX/FORTRAN automatically detects the potential for vector and parallel processing in standard Fortran code and generates instructions that use the concurrency and vectorization features of the hardware to full advantage (see Chapter 3).

At compile time, FX/FORTRAN permits the programmer to control the optimization process at the program (global), subprogram, and loop levels while providing feedback on the optimization process.

FX/FORTRAN is an ANSI standard FORTRAN-77 compiler that contains most of the extensions of VAX/VMS FORTRAN-77 and other industry-standard compilers. In addition, FX/FORTRAN extends the language to permit assignment and other operations on full arrays and the use of full arrays in intrinsic functions. These extensions make source codes simpler and more structured, as well as help to clarify the intent of the programmer to the compiler. The extensions closely follow the proposed updates to the Fortran standard contained in Standing Document 8, Version 101, of the ANSI X3J3 Committee (published August 1986), also known as the FORTRAN-8X committee.

FX/FORTRAN is capable of generating code that executes in five different modes.

1. A *scalar* is a single element or value, such as S, A(I), or 1.0. *Scalar processing* uses instructions that operate on single elements or data at any one time. Each

CE has a full-scalar instruction set that operates on both 32- and 64-bit data elements.

2. A *vector* is a series of elements, such as all the elements of the array A, or every fourth element of the array B. *Vector processing* uses instructions that operate on an entire vector. Each CE supports a full 64-bit vector processing instruction set.

3. In *scalar-concurrent* mode, each of up to eight CEs in the computational complex continuously executes the next available iteration of a loop until the entire loop has been executed. In some cases, hardware synchronization mechanisms are automatically employed to synchronize dependencies between loops. As a result, loops that would be forced to run in serial mode on traditional vector computers often can be optimized for scalar-concurrent execution on the Alliant.

4. *Vector-concurrent mode* is similar to scalar-concurrent except that each CE operates on up to 32 iterations of a loop using its vector hardware. With eight CEs simultaneously operating on a full vector of 32 elements, a 256-element vector can be processed in the time it takes to execute a single 32-element vector.

5. Where loops are nested, FX/FORTRAN generates executable code that runs the innermost loop in vector mode and the next outer loop in concurrent mode. Taken as a whole, the two loops run in *concurrent-outer-vector-inner mode* (COVI). An array operation within a loop also executes in COVI mode. The array operation executes in vector mode; the loop iterations run concurrently. An array operation on a multidimensional array also executes in COVI mode. The leftmost dimension executes in vector mode; the next dimension executes in concurrent mode.

FIGURE 7.12. FX/FORTRAN optimization (courtesy of Alliant Computer Sys. Corp.).

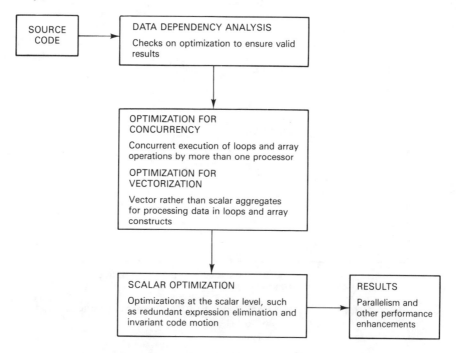

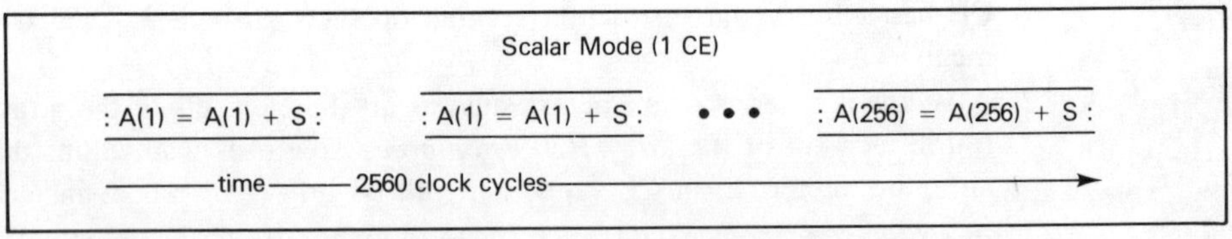

Scalar Mode (1 CE)

: A(1) = A(1) + S :   : A(1) = A(1) + S :   • • •   : A(256) = A(256) + S :

————time——— 2560 clock cycles————————————————→

With vectorization and concurrency optimizations turned off, FX/Fortran generates code that executes the loop in scalar (or serial) mode on a single CE with each iteration executed after the previous one completes.

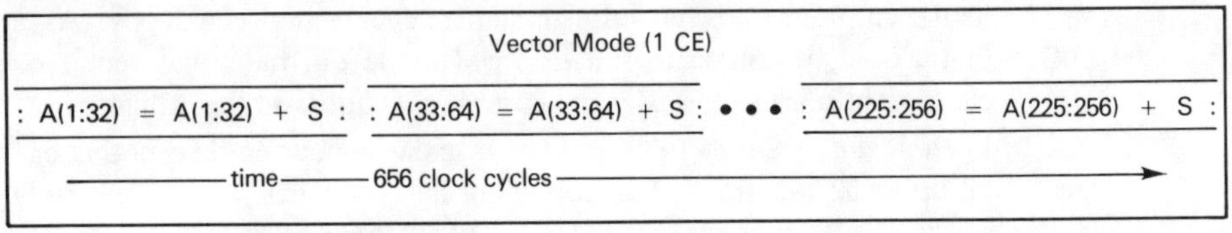

Vector Mode (1 CE)

: A(1:32) = A(1:32) + S :   : A(33:64) = A(33:64) + S : • • • : A(225:256) = A(225:256) + S :

————————time——— 656 clock cycles————————————————→

With concurrency turned off, FX-Fortran generates code that executes the loop in vector mode with eight vector instructions executed serially on a single CE. Each vector instruction works on 32 iterations of the loop.

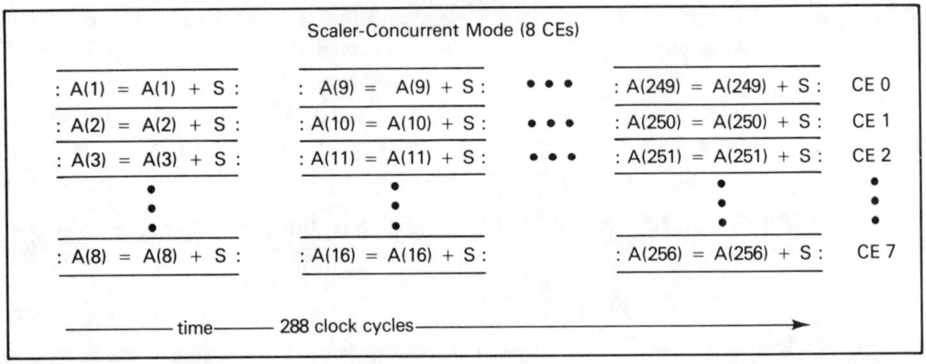

Scaler-Concurrent Mode (8 CEs)

: A(1) = A(1) + S :	: A(9) = A(9) + S :	• • •	: A(249) = A(249) + S :	CE 0
: A(2) = A(2) + S :	: A(10) = A(10) + S :	• • •	: A(250) = A(250) + S :	CE 1
: A(3) = A(3) + S :	: A(11) = A(11) + S :	• • •	: A(251) = A(251) + S :	CE 2
•	•		•	•
•	•		•	•
: A(8) = A(8) + S :	: A(16) = A(16) + S :		: A(256) = A(256) + S :	CE 7

————————time——— 288 clock cycles————————————————→

With vectorization turned off, FX/Fortran generates code that executes the loop in scalar-concurrent mode with each iteration of the loop being executed on a separate CE.

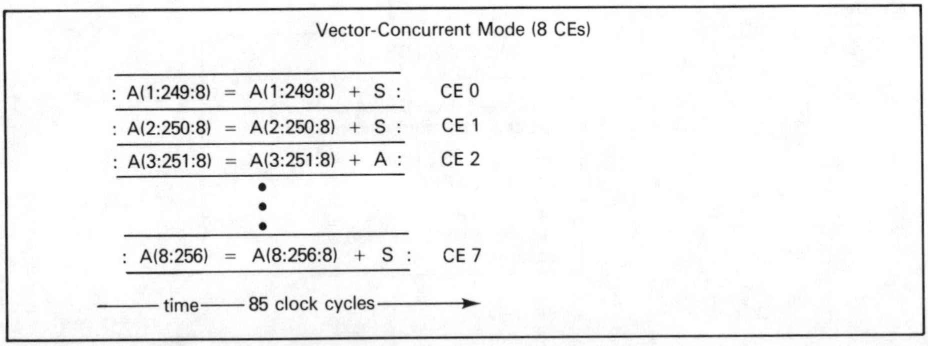

Vector-Concurrent Mode (8 CEs)

: A(1:249:8) = A(1:249:8) + S :	CE 0
: A(2:250:8) = A(2:250:8) + S :	CE 1
: A(3:251:8) = A(3:251:8) + A :	CE 2
•	
•	
•	
: A(8:256) = A(8:256:8) + S :	CE 7

————time——— 85 clock cycles————→

With full optimization, FX/Fortran generates code that executes the loop in vector-concurrent mode making direct use of both vector and parallel processing.

FIGURE 7.13. FORTRAN code generation for different optimization modes (courtesy of Alliant Computer Sys. Corp.).

Concurrent-Outer-Vector-Inner Mode (8 CEs)		
: A(1:32,1) = A(1:32,1) + S :	: A(225:256,1) = A(225:256,1) + S :	CE 0
: A(1:32,2) = A(1:32,2) + S :	: A(225:256,2) = A(225:256,2) + S :	CE 1
: A(1:32,3) = A(1:32,3) + S :	: A(225:256,3) = A(225:256,3) + S :	CE 2
: A(1:32,4) = A(1:32,4) + S :	: A(225:256,4) = A(225:256,4) + S :	CE 3
: A(1:32,5) = A(1:32,5) + S :	: A(225:256,5) = A(225:256,5) + S :	CE 4
: A(1:32,6) = A(1:32,6) + S :	: A(225:256,6) = A(225:256,6) + S :	CE 5
: A(1:32,7) = A(1:32,7) + S :	: A(225:256,7) = A(225:256,7) + S :	CE 6
: A(1:32,8) = A(1:32,8) + S :	: A(225:256,8) = A(225:256,8) + S :	CE 7

FIGURE 7.14. Nested loop COVI optimization (courtesy of Alliant Computer Sys. Corp.).

FX /FORTRAN optimizes programs for concurrency, vectorization, and scalar (global) performance. The compiler analyzes programs for data dependencies and generates optimized executable code that can run on the computational complex or any detached CE (see Figure 7.12).

FX/FORTRAN compiler optimizes the following operations for vectorization and concurrency:

1. DO loops execute in vector-concurrent mode unless they contain restricted statements or data dependencies, in which case they may execute in vector mode or scalar-concurrent mode depending on the nature of the restrictions or dependencies. Array operations execute in vector-concurrent mode except that concurrency may be limited due to restrictions or data dependencies.

2. Nested DO loops and multidimensional array operations run in vector-concurrent or concurrent-out-vector-inner-mode.

3. DO WHILE loops run in scalar-concurrent mode.

Figure 7.13 shows how FX/FORTRAN generates code to execute a simple DO loop in scalar, vector, scalar-concurrent, and vector-concurrent modes.

Figure 7.14 is an example showing nested loops in which the inner loop executes in vector mode and the outer loop is executed concurrently. Consider the following loop:

$$DO \quad 10 \quad J = 1.8$$
$$DO \quad 10 \quad I = 1.256$$
$$10 \quad A(I,J) = A(I,J) + S$$

which also can be written in ANSI 8X syntax as:

$$A (1:256, 1:8) = A (1:256, 1:8) + S$$

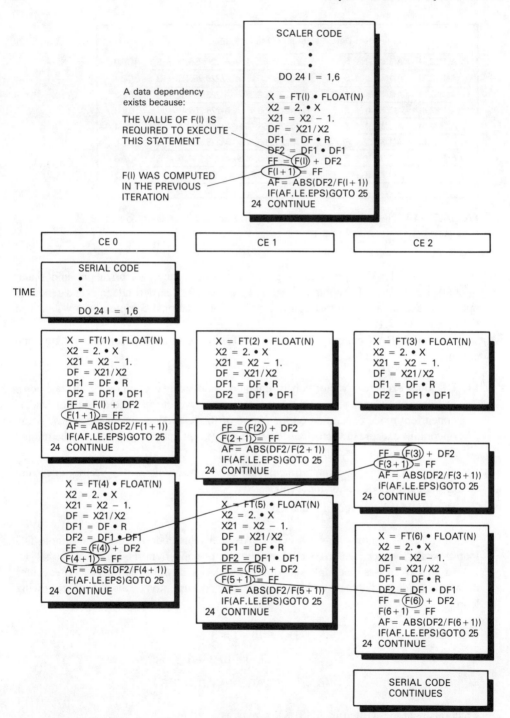

FIGURE 7.15. Loop parallelization (courtesy of Alliant Computer Sys. Corp.).

FX/FORTRAN automatically compiles either of the above in concurrent-outer-vector-inner (COVI) mode. Another example of loop parallelization is illustrated in Figure 7.15. The FX/FORTRAN compiler contains a broad range of *global optimization* capabilities that are *automatically* performed on source code when the global optimization option is enabled by the user. Some of the capabilities are:

- constant computation and propagation;
- redundant expression elimination;
- global register allocation for frequently used variables;
- dead store elimination; and
- others.

The FX/FORTRAN has extensions that provide compatibility with DEC (VAX/VMS), Cray, IBM, and other environments. Porting existing FORTRAN programs, developed on other systems, to Alliant, requires little effort.

References 1. J. P. Hayes, *Computer Organization and Architecture, 2nd. ed.*, McGraw-Hill, NY, 1988.

2. K. Hwang, F. A. Briggs, *Computer Architecture and Parallel Processing*, McGraw-Hill, NY, 1984.

3. S. G. Tucker, "The IBM 3090 System: An Overview," *IBM Systems Journal*, Vol. 25, No. 1, pp. 4–19, 1986.

4. W. Buchholz, ed., *Planning a Computer System*: *Project Stretch*, McGraw-Hill, NY, 1962.

5. *Alliant FX/Series Product Summary*, Alliant Computer Systems Corp., Dec. 1988.

6. *MC68020 32-Bit Microprocessor User's Manual, 2nd. ed.*, Prentice-Hall, Englewood Cliffs, NJ, 1985.

7. *FX/Series Architectural Manual*, Alliant Computer System Corp., 300–0001–B, Jan. 1986.

8. R. L. Brown, P. J. Denning, W. F. Tichy, "Advanced Operating Systems," *IEEE Computer*, Vol. 17, No. 10, pp. 173–190, Oct. 1984.

9. A. Silberschatz, J. L. Peterson, *Operating Systems Concepts, alternate ed.*, Addison Wesley, Reading MA, 1988.

10. *FX/FORTRAN Programmer's Handbook*, Alliant Computer Systems Corp., 302–00001–C, March 1987.

CHAPTER 8

Bus-oriented Systems

8.1 The ELXSI System

The ELXSI System 6400 features up to 12 CPUs, connected to a single system bus called the *Gigabus* [1–3]. A block diagram of the ELXSI System 6400 is shown in Figure 8.1. The 6400 uses ELXSI proprietary, custom-made, 64-bit CPUs, realized on ECL VLSI gate array boards. Three types of CPUs are offered. The 6410 is made up of ALU a *Floating Point Accelerator* (FPA), and Cache (16 KBytes) circuit cards. The 6420 is made up of the Instruction Unit, Execution Unit, and the Storage Unit (64 KBytes cache). While the Instruction Unit performs instruction decode and branch calculations, the Execution Unit performs floating point, integer, and ASCII operations. The Storage Unit performs bus communication, virtual address translation, and data/process storage. The 6460 is the top model; it outperforms the 6420 by a factor of 3.5. All three models have the same architecture. The performance of the 6410 CPU is 4 VAX MIPS, while that of the 6420 is 7.6 VAX MIPS. The performance of the 6460 is 25 VAX MIPS scalar and 10 MFLOPS (64-bit Linpack).

All of the above models can be interconnected to the same bus and different models can coexist in the same system. Up to 12 6410 and/or 6420 CPUs and up to 10 6460 CPUs can be configured in a single system. A system composed of 6460s is also known as a *Superframe*.

The CPUs implement the IEEE *Standard Floating Point* formats of 32 and 64 bits and an extended 80-bits format. Each CPU has 16 sets of 16 64-bit general purpose registers in the Instruction Unit, and 16 sets of process context registers in the *Process Context Cache*. The Storage Unit also contains a 16×128 *Translation Lookaside Buffer* (TLB) for virtual to physical address translation in the 6410 and 6420, and a 16K entries TLB in the 6460.

The Gigabus is a proprietary 110-bit (64-bit data path), 25 nsec cycle time bus. Its top bandwidth is 320 MBytes/sec. To compare: the DEC VAXBI offers 13MBytes/sec at 100 nsec cycle time.

The 6400 offers an overall virtual address space of four GBytes, with two GBytes per user program space. The physical memory is available with increments of 16, 32 or 64 MBytes, up to two GBytes. The I/O space is managed by up to four I/O Processors (IOP) with a bandwidth of 16 MBytes/sec per IOP.

The 6460 model handles a 512 KByte instruction and a 512 KByte data cache, for a total of one MByte cache storage.

The ELXSI offers a virtual machine interface called the *System Foundation*. It is a collection of 25 processes that offer the user a number of concurrent OS environments. The System Foundation manages process creation, process deletion, virtual memory,

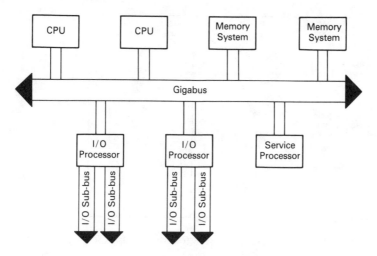

FIGURE 8.1. Components of the ELXSI System 6400 (courtesy of ELXSI Corp.).

message-passing between processes, device access, and CPU scheduling. Each of the System Foundation processes communicates with the other processes and with the respective OS by sending a message or packet over the Gigabus. System Foundation processes also communicate with device controllers, such as IOPs, by sending or receiving messages because the IOP appears to the OS as just another process. The System Foundation also supports real-time processing.

The OS environments offered by ELXSI are:

(a) EMBOS (Elxsi Message-Based OS)—a native ELXSI proprietary OS.

(b) EMS (Elxsi eMulation System)—an extension of EMBOS that emulates the DEC VMS, permitting VAX users (under VMS) to run on the 6400 and network with VAX hosts. EMS provides DCL, run-time libraries, EDT editor, and Decnet.

(c) AT & T UNIX System V.3.

(d) Berkeley UNIX 4.3 BSD.

The processes on the ELXSI intercommunicate and are synchronized through a message-passing system (see Chapter 4) [3]. The basic elements of the EMBOS message system are *links* and *funnels* (see Figure 8.2). Messages are sent on links and received on funnels. Each link and each funnel is owned by exactly one process. Each process can have up to 65,535 links and 255 funnels. Each link points into exactly one funnel, but a single funnel can have many links pointing into it. A link can point into a funnel in the same process or another process. A link pointing into a funnel that belongs to the same process is called a *self-link*. Most links point into funnels in other processes, and are used to send messages to those processes. Since each link points to exactly one funnel, it also points to exactly one process. Links can be copied and passed from one process to another, but each copy of a link still points into the same funnel as the original. Once a link points into a particular funnel, that funnel cannot be changed.

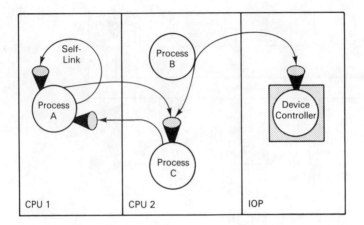

FIGURE 8.2. Links, funnels, and processes (courtesy of ELXSI Corp.).

The links for a process are kept in a *link table*, and the funnels in a *funnel table*. Link and funnel IDs are indexes that select a particular entry in the appropriate table. These tables cannot be modified or accessed directly, but a process can read individual entries in its link and funnel tables with special intrinsics. A link table entry, for example, contains the process ID and the funnel number into which the link points.

ELXSI provides compilers for FORTRAN 77, Lisp, C, Pascal, Prolog, Ada, Cobol, and an Assembler. To aide in parallelizing code, ELXSI provides a set of software tools, called *Parallel Intrinsics*, that users can call from within an application program. These intrinsics include calls to share common memory between programs, create a "child" process (in a tree-like structure), and process locks on shared memory. ELXSI has announced plans to offer an integrated vectorizing FORTRAN compiler with VMS extension.

8.2 The Sequent Balance and Symmetry Systems

The Sequent Computer Systems, Inc. has two families of multiprocessors: the *Balance* [4–7] *Series* and the *Symmetry Series*. The balance series is abbreviated by a "B" and the Symmetry Series by an "S." These two series are very similar in their structure, configuration, OS, and user software. The primary difference between them is the micro-processor used is one of a number of processors. The B series uses the National Semicon-ductor NS32032 (the more advanced NS32332 or NS32532 may be used in the future), while the S series uses the Intel 80386. Thus, the system architecture, at the assembly, or the machine language level, is substantially different for the two series. However, as far as the *High-level Language* (HLL) user is concerned, the two series present a very similar view. There are, of course, differences in speed, performance, memory size, and other points.

Each series has two basic models. The Balance series has B8 with up to 12 CPUs and B21 with up to 30 CPUs. The Symmetry series has S27 with up to 10 CPUs and S81 with up to 30 CPUs. Some of the principal system parameters are summarized as follows:

	Balance (NS32032)		Symmetry (I80386)	
	B8	B21	S27	S81
Number of CPUs	2–12	4–30	2–10	2–30
Cache per CPU (KBytes)	8	8	64	64
Physical Memory (MBytes)	2–28	2–28	8–80	8–240
Virtual Address Space per				
process (MBytes)	16	16	256	256
Dual-channel Disk Controller				
(two channel/controller)	0–1	1–4	0–1	1–4
Asynchronous Ports	16–96	16–256	16–96	16–256
MULTIBUS Slots	7–16	12–48	7–16	12–48
System Performance (MIPS)	1.5–8.4	3–21	6–27	6–81

All of the CPU units have a *Floating Point Unit* (FPU) (NS32081 for the B series, 80387 for the S series), and a *Memory Management Unit* (MMU) (NS32082 for the B series, and the 80386 chip for S), as a standard feature. Optionally, a *Floating Point Accelerator* (Weitek 1167-based) can be added for each CPU on the S series.

All of the above systems offer the same software features:

Standard: DYNIX OS
        C compiler
        Parallel programming tools
        TCP/IP networking
Optional: FORTRAN 77
        ANSI Pascal
        Sequent Network File System (NFS)

All of the above systems are configured around a single *system bus* (80 MByte/ sec.), as shown in Figure 8.3. The following subsystems are interconnected to the system bus:

1. Dual CPU processor boards;

2. Memory Controller and Memory Expansion boards;

3. Small Computer System Interface (SCSI) controller, interconnecting to peripherals (tapes, disks);

4. Ethernet interface;

5. Diagnostics processor interface;

6. Dual-channel disk controller interface;

7. Multibus adapter board and interface. Peripherals are connected to the available Multibus units.

Each CPU and each board on the system bus, on all systems, has a proprietary integrated circuit, called the *System Link and Interrupt Controller* (SLIC) chip, whose task is to manage the control of multiple processors. All SLICs are connected by a bit-serial data path called the *SLIC bus*. Together, the SLICs manage interprocessor communication, synchronized access to kernel data structures, distribution of interrupts among

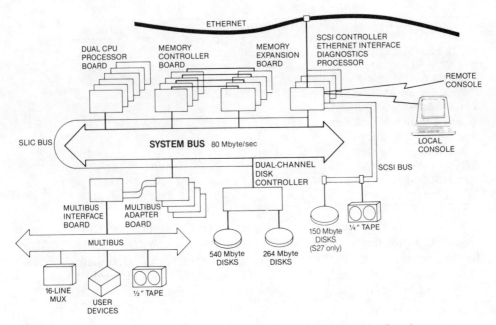

FIGURE 8.3. The Sequent System (courtesy of Sequent Computer Sys. Corp.).

CPUs, and diagnostic and configuration control. The SLIC mechanism is similar to the corresponding mechanism in the proposed IEEE 896 Futurebus [8]. The SLIC bus uses a high-speed, synchronous, bit-serial protocol, independent of the system bus. All SLIC communication is in the form of command-response packets of fixed length.

Each B series CPU has an 8 KByte, two-way, set-associative cache. The cached data is organized into 512 rows each containing 8-byte blocks. A *write-through* policy is adopted. That is, when an item stored in cache is updated (written into), the corresponding memory location is updated at the next cycle while the CPU continues with the next operation. All boards monitor the system bus, and if any other CPU's cache contains a copy of the block that has been overwritten, that copy is marked as out of date.

The S series cache (for each CPU) is 64-KByte, two-way set-associative. Contrary to the B series, a *write-back* (copy-back) policy is adopted. That is, a whole block is updated in main memory when that block is being replaced in the cache. Cache coherency (see Chapter 5) is maintained by the following procedure: When CPU A loads data into its cache that are also held in another CPU's cache, both cache controllers mark the data as shared. If CPU A then writes to one of the cached locations, A's cache controller broadcasts a message on the system bus, declaring that if any other user is caching this location, that user's data are now invalid. Until the new data are written back to main memory, any references to the location will be served by CPU A's cache [7].

The DYNIX OS is implemented on all of the sequent series systems. It is dual-universe OS, originally derived from UNIX 4.2 BSD. The DYNIX *att* universe is compatible with UNIX System V, version 2, release 2. The *ucb* universe is compatible with UNIX 4.2 BSD, and also includes enhancements from UNIX 4.3 BSD. Both universes may coexist on the same Sequent system.

The DYNIX supports any number of CPUs. To add CPUs to an existing system, one shuts it down, inserts one or more additional dual-processor boards, and starts the system back up. The system takes inventory of its resources (CPUs, memory, and peripheral devices) at startup time. No modifications to the OS or to user applications are required. CPUs can be removed with similar ease.

DYNIX supports parallelization and functional partitioning in all of the HLLs offered by the system. The parallelization is not entirely automatic however. The user has to analize the program and insert appropriate directives [6]. Sequent supports a fully validated Ada development capability.

8.3 The Encore Multimax

The Encore Multimax system uses National Semiconductor microprocessors as CPUs [9, 10], as did the Sequent Balance system. A block diagram of the Multimax is shown

FIGURE 8.4. Multimax system functional diagram (courtesy of Encore Computer Corp.).

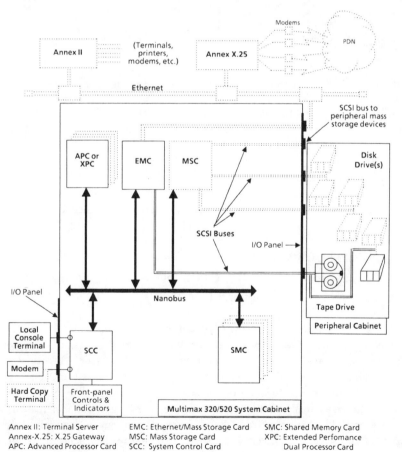

Annex II: Terminal Server
Annex-X.25: X.25 Gateway
APC: Advanced Processor Card

EMC: Ethernet/Mass Storage Card
MSC: Mass Storage Card
SCC: System Control Card

SMC: Shared Memory Card
XPC: Extended Perfomance
    Dual Processor Card

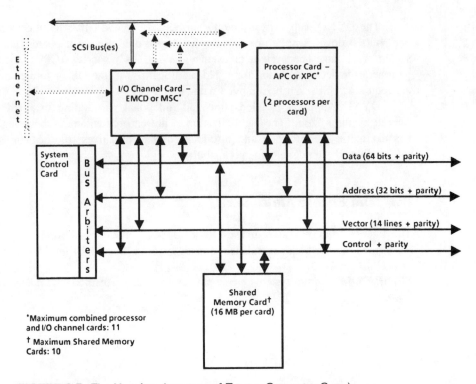

FIGURE 8.5. The Nanobus (courtesy of Encore Computer Corp.).

in Figure 8.4. The Multimax 310 and 320 use the NS32332, and the Multimax 510 and 520 use the NS32532. The discussion of this section will concentrate on the current top product, the Multimax 520.

The system is configured around a single, synchronous, non-multiplexed bus, called the *Nanobus*, shown in Figure 8.5. Its data bandwidth is 100 MBytes/sec. It has a 64-bit data path and a separate 32-bit address path.

From two to 20 CPUs (two per Extended-Performance Processor Card (XPC) can be configured. A processor unit contains:

• An NS32532 (30 MHz) CPU;

• An NS32381 Floating Point Unit (FPU); and

• An Integral Memory Management Unit (MMU).

A block diagram of an XPC card is shown in Figure 8.6. Each CPU has a 256 KByte, 35*n*sec access cache memory that uses a write-deferred protocol. This protocol writes data to cache rather than main memory by withholding main memory writes until the last possible moment. That is, until the cache must be purged or cache usage protocol requires that the stored location be replaced with a different one. Such locations can be written and read many times before being replaced, and, for that reason, accesses to them practically disappear from the nanobus. Coherency is maintained across caches by a special system of ownership. Sharing, whereby the cache to which an entry is

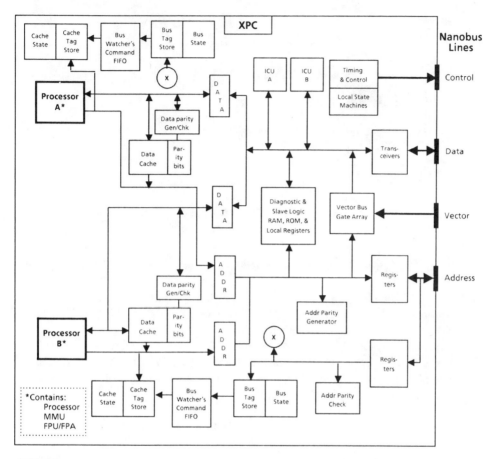

FIGURE 8.6. Extended performance processor card block diagram (courtesy of Encore Computer Corp.).

being written, must first attain ownership of that location, thus causing any other caches sharing the data to mark their copies invalid. It must then assume the responsibility of providing the changed data to any other cache that subsequently wishes to read it. Finally, it must mark its copy invalid if any other cache requests ownership.

Write deferred cache protocol, in conjunction with the 256K byte cache size used on current Encore processor cards, allows a theoretical aggregate system speed of 200 MIPS (providing acceptable headroom for the 120+ MIPS maximum speed of current Encore systems). The main memory can be configured up to 160 Mbytes. Up to 67.2 Gigabytes of disk capacity is available, along with up to 16 6250/1600 BPI nine-track tape drives.

The peak advertised performance of the Multimax 520 is 170 MIPS. The following OS environments are offered:

1. UMAX V, derived from AT & T UNIX System V.2, version 4, compatible with System V Interface definition.

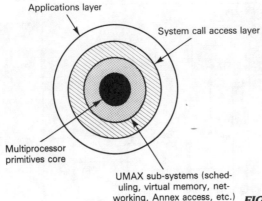

UMAX sub-systems (sched-
uling, virtual memory, net-
working, Annex access, etc.)   ***FIGURE 8.7.*** UMAX layering (courtesy of
Encore Computer Corp.).

2. UMAX 4.2, derived from UNIX 4.2 BSD, developed at the University of California
   at Berkeley.

3. The MACH multiprocessor-oriented OS, developed at the Carnegie-Mellon University
   and ported to Encore under a DARPA contract (see subsection 4.5.3). The MACH
   OS undergoes further development at Encore.

    The UMAX OS is structured in four layers as shown in Figure 8.7. The UMAX
OS provides the following synchronization mechanisms between UMAX processes and
Multimax hardware (see Chapter 4):

(a) *Spin Locks* execute instruction loops until the expected condition occurs. Used
    only for critical, short duration events.

(b) *Semaphores* suspend a process until the resource it needs is available (see Chapter
    3).

(c) *Read/Write Locks* (UMAX 4.2 only) control access to data structures for a
    single writer or multiple readers. Read/write locks are special semaphores that
    prohibit write access until all pending reads are complete, and prohibit read
    access while any write is either pending or in progress.

    The UMAX OS supports communication protocols for network interconnection
using the Annex as shown in Figures 8.8 and 8.9. The Annex uses the Arpanet suite
of communication protocols. It also became a de facto standard for Ethernet communication
[11]. Figure 8.8 shows the relationships between the protocol elements used by the
Annex. They are shown in order of increasing generality from top to bottom. The
more specific (higher level) protocols use the services provided by the lower level ones.
The tty semantics, rdp network asynchronous serial interfaces, rlogin, routed, rwho,
eprc protocols are Berkeley or Encore additions to the Arpanet suite.

    The High-level Languages supported are: C, Pascal, FORTRAN 77, Basic, Ada,
Cobol, and Lisp. The parallel FORTRAN programming tools package allows for automatic
and/or user-specified parallelism. It includes a parallelizing compiler, optimizer, analysis

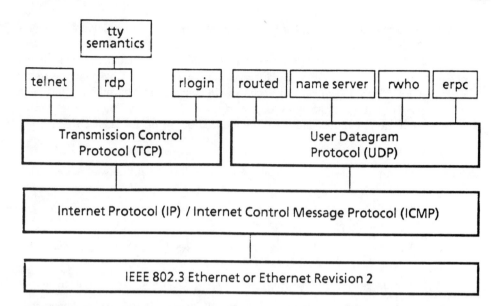

FIGURE 8.8. Protocols used by the annex (courtesy of Encore Computer Corp.).

and transformation tools, and language extensions. The parallel optimizer in the package was developed by Kuck and Associates and enhanced by Encore. Encore's parallel implementation of Ada runs on the Multimax, delivering parallel processing to both Ada development and execution.

Another potential Encore product, envisaged in the future, is the Gigamax, consisting of a set of Multimax systems (clusters), sharing a common bus [10]. This product is targeted to have up to 1000 MIPS performance. Any byte of memory in any of the Multimax systems can be directly addressed by any processor in the Gigamax. The

FIGURE 8.9. The encore distributed computing environment (courtesy of Encore Computer Corp.).

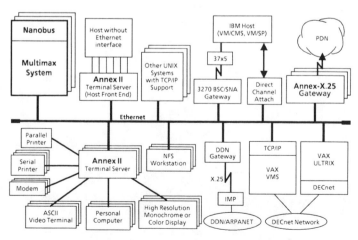

Gigamax contains a *Global Switch* which is a specially constructed version of the Nanobus. There is an *Ultra Interface Card* (UIC), which plugs into the *Global Switch*. Associated with the UIC is the *Ultra Cache Card* (UCC) that contains a cache associated with a Multimax cluster. A large Gigamax can be constructed by plugging in 8 UICs into a Global Bus, and connecting each to a UIC plugged into a Multimax cluster. The resulting system will be eight times as powerful as a Multimax. The envisaged size of the UCC is 16 to 32 MBytes and it will be realized out of off the shelf DRAMS.

References   1. J. A. Steinberg, "A Virtual VAX does it in Parallel," *Digital Review*, March 23, 1987, pp. 2–5.

2. J. Sanguinetti, "Performance of a Message-based Multiprocessor," *IEEE Computer*, Vol. 19, No. 9, pp. 47–55, Sept. 1986.

3. R. Olson, "Parallel Processing in a Message-based Operating System," *IEEE Software*, Vol. 2, pp. 39–49, July 1985.

4. *Balance Technical Summary*, *MAN-0110-0*, Sequent Computer Systems, Inc. Nov. 1986.

5. S. Thakkar, P. Grifford, G. Fielland, "Balance: A Shared Memory Multiprocessor System," *Proc. 2nd. Int. Conf. on Supercomputers*, ICS 87, Vol. 1, pp. 93–101, Santa Clara, CA, May 4–8, 1987.

6. A. Osterhaug, *Guide to Parallel Programming on Sequent Computer Systems*, Sequent Computer Systems Inc., 1986.

7. R. Wilson, "Increased CPU Speed Drives Changes in Multiprocessor Cache and Bus Designs," *Computer Design*, June 15, 1987, p. 20.

8. M. Smolin, "Microstandards," *IEEE MICRO*, Vol. 7, No. 3, p. 85, June 1987.

9. Encore Computer Corp., *Multimax Technical Summary*, *726–01759 Rev'd*, March 1987.

10. I. R. Nassi, "A Preliminary Report on the Ultramax: A Massively Parallel Shared Memory Multiprocessor," *Report ETR 87–004*, Encore Computer Corp., 1987.

11. J. B. Pastel, *Internet Protocol Approaches*, *in Computer Network Architectrues and Protocols*, P. E. Green, Jr., ed., pp. 511–526, Plenum Press, NY, 1982.

CHAPTER 9

Cube Systems

9.1 The NCUBE

The basic hypercube structure was introduced in Chapter 2 and is illustrated in Figure 9.1 [1–6]. The NCUBE Corporation has developed a commercial system, configured as a hypercube, or n-cube with 2**n processor nodes. Three products are offered:

- NCUBE/4 with up to four processing nodes (2**2).
- NCUBE/7 with up to 128 processing nodes (2**7).
- NCUBE/10 with up to 1024 processing nodes (2**10).

The current discussion will concentrate on the top product, the NCUBE/10. All of the above systems use the same processor node.

The NCUBE individual CPU is a proprietary, custom-made, two-micron NMOS, 160000 transistors, 68-pin chip. Its instruction set and operand modes are very similar to those of the DEC VAX. Each CPU performs at two MIPS (10 MHz) and 0.5 MFLOPS (32-bit, IEEE Standard). Each CPU node has 512 KBytes of local memory. Thus, the total amount of memory of the NCUBE/10 is 512 MBytes. The processing part consist of 16 processor boards (16″ × 22″), each of which contain 64 nodes and 32 MBytes of memory, as illustrated in Figure 9.1. The backplane connections of each board consist of 640 connections (512 hypercube interconnect and 128 I/O) just for communication channels. The I/O part contains 8 I/O boards. At least one of the I/O boards must be a *host board* (Intel 80286 + 4 MBytes RAM) to run the OS. The host memory can be used as a shared memory by other IOPs.

Each I/O board has 128 bidirectional channels directly connected to a subcube of the hypercube. Each I/O board contains 16 NCUBE CPU chips, each of which serves as an IOP and is connected to eight nodes in the main hypercube. As the hypercube node CPUs, an IOP has a 128 KBytes RAM that occupies a fixed slot in the 80286 host's four MBytes memory space.

There is no shared memory in the n-cube system, and, in that respect, it does not conform to the Enslow definition of a multiprocessor (see Chapter 1). Values of parameters and any other type of information are shared between the nodes by *message passing* (see Chapter 4) along the communication lines. The node CPU communicates with other nodes by means of asynchronous DMA operations over 22 bit-serial I/O lines. These I/O lines are paired into 11 bidirectional channels which permit the formation

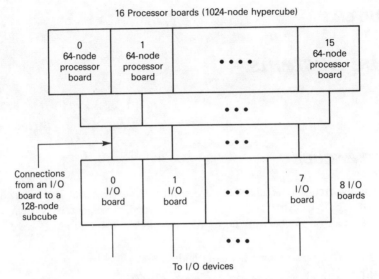

FIGURE 9.1. The NCUBE/10 system (courtesy of NCUBE Corp.).

of a 10-cube and allow one channel to interconnect to an I/O board. Each node-to-node channel operates at 10 MHz, yielding a data transfer rate of one MBytes/sec. per channel in each direction.

A proprietary UNIX-like OS, the Axis, has been developed. It is particularly geared to manage the main cube array. The system supports compilers for FORTRAN 77 and C, and a parallel debugger which facilitates the debugging of programs running on a hypercube array.

9.2   The Intel iPSC

The Intel iPSC (personal supercomputer) and iPSC/2 systems [6–8] are n-cube systems offering n=5, 6, and 7 options. That is, they can be optionally configured for 32, 64, or 128 nodes processors. The iPSC system consists of two major parts:

1. The *Cube*, consisting of the hypercube node processors and their interconnections.
2. The *Cube Manager*, Intel System 286/310, which serves as the local host for the Cube. It provides interface to users, OS running, compilation, program loading, error handling and system diagnostics control. It includes the 80286 CPU, the 80287 Numeric Coprocessor and up to four MBytes physical memory (with expansion option).

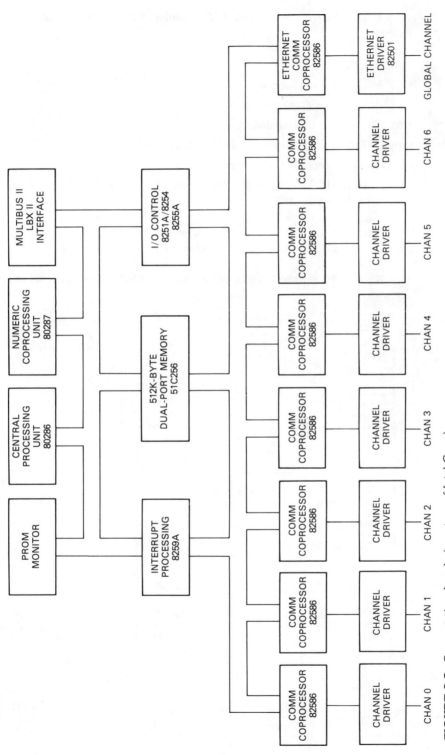

FIGURE 9.2. Computational node (courtesy of Intel Corp.).

105

Each cube *node* (see Figure 9.2) is mounted on a 9 × 11 inch Eurocard, which includes:

- 80286 CPU.
- 80287 Numeric Coprocessor.
- 512 KByte Dual Port Dynamic RAM.
- 64 KByte PROM (expandable).
- eight 82568 local area network (LAN) coprocessors:
  —seven for internode communication;
  —one connects through an 82501 Ethernet Driver to the *Global Channel*, 10 MBit/ sec., Ethernet IEEE 802.3.

The LAN coprocessors are connected to the CPU through an 8259A Interrupt unit. The Manager-to-Cube communications channels are shown in Figure 9.3.

FIGURE 9.3. Manager-to-Cube communication channels (courtesy of Intel Corp.).

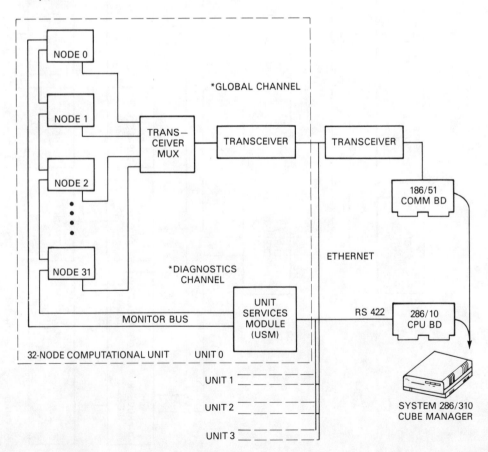

Some of the iPSC properties can be summarized as follows:

iPSC model	5-cube	6-cube	7-cube
Processing nodes	32	64	128
Total memory, MBytes	16	32	64
Communication channels	80	192	448
Performance, MIPS	25	50	100
Performance, MFLOPS	2	4	8
Performance, KWhetstones/sec	5,750	11,500	23,000
Aggregate memory bandwidth (MByte/sec)	512	1,024	2,048
Aggregate communication bandwidth (MByte/sec)	64	128	256
Aggregate messages (Kmessages/sec)	180	360	720

The iPSC/2 has a structure identical to that of the iPSC. However, its node contains the 32-bit 80386 as the CPU, the 80387 floating point accelerator and up to 16 MBytes memory. Thus, for a maximum 128 node configuration the total conceivable iPSC/2 memory is 16 MBytes$*$128 $=$ 2$**$31 Bytes $=$ two GBytes. At the moment, only up to eight MBytes/node are allowed for the 128-node configuration. Therefore, the current available maximal total memory is one GBytes. The iPSC/2 Manager is also 80386-based and features eight MBytes of memory, a 140 MByte hard disk, and an Ethernet connection [9].

There is an optional *Scalar Extension* (SX) module to the iPSC/2 node, based upon a Weitek 1167 floating point unit. It triples the node performance capability.

A recent extension of the iPSC, called the *Vector Extension*, iPSC-VX contains an ensemble of node processors, supported by a high-performance *Vector Coprocessor* board (an example is Vortex, from Sky Computers) that occupies the adjacent card slot in the system. A private iLBX (iLBX-2 for iPSC/2) bus connects the two boards (node and vector coprocessor) in a tightly coupled, shared-memory interface which is, transparent to the user. Each VX vector-extended iPSC/2 node obtains peak performance that exceeds six MFLOPS double- and 20 MFLOPS single-precision. The aggregate peak performance for a 64-node system, VX-extended, is 424 MFLOPS double- and 1280 MFLOP single-precision. The overall 128-node iPSC/2 performance is 512 MIPS [9].

The iPSC OS is the Xenix 3.0, a derivative of UNIX system III including enhancements from Berkeley, Microsoft and Intel, supporting FORTRAN 77 and C. Each iPSC/2 node carries its own multitasking OS (see Chapter 4) called *Node Executive*/2 (NX/2). The NX/2 supports multiprocessing with round-robin scheduling in each iPSC/2 node. The NX/2 loader takes UNIX Common Object File Format files as input. NX/2 supports UNIX-style standard I/O at the node. The NX/2 uses the 80386 processor to provide each process with a separate memory space [10]. The FORTRAN 77, C, and Concurrent Common Lisp are supported on the iPSC/2.

9.3 The Floating Point Systems (FPS) T-series

The FPS T-series can be expanded, on a modular basis, into a 14-cube system, with 16384 nodes and a peak overall performance of 262 GFLOPS, if all nodes are kept busy all the time [6,7,11,12].

Each node of the T-series is mounted on a single board. It contains:

1. An INMOS Transputer, IMS T414, acting as the CPU. It is a 32-bit system with two KBytes RAM on chip, and an addressing capability of four GBytes (32 address bits). Internal, on chip, memory access is one clock cycle. Off chip memory is three cycles. Peak performance is 7 MIPS.

2. Two six-stage, pipelined, vector, floating point processors, operating concurrently with the CPU. One vector processor is an adder, the other, a multiplier. Both work with IEEE Standard formats, performing a 64-bit floating point operation every 125 *n*sec.

3. Two register banks—bank A:256 KBytes and bank B:768 KBytes, for a total of 1024 KBytes—constituting a dual ported, dynamic 1 MByte RAM.

4. Multiplexer of the four bidirectional communication links of the CPU into 16 bidirectional links (one MBytes/sec, each direction, four active at a time).

The peak floating point performance of each node is 12 MFLOPS. Eight nodes form a *module*, and two modules (16 nodes) form a *cabinet*. The systems, configured in the T-series are labeled *T/noct*, where noct is the number of nodes in octal. Some examples of system configurations and their peak performance are:

System	Nodes	Cabinets	Performance
T/20	16	1	192 MFLOPS
T/40	32	2	384 MFLOPS
T/100	64	4	768 MFLOPS
T/200	128	8	1.5 GFLOPS
T/400	256	16	3.0 GFLOPS
T/1000	512	32	6.1 GFLOPS
T/2000	1024	64	12.3 GFLOPS
T/40000	16364	1024	262 GFLOPS

A MicroVAXII serves as a host computer to run the OS, utilities, and to provide a DECnet interface to a networked environment. The DEC Ultrix OS is implemented. The *T-series Program Development Software* (TPDS) includes FORTRAN and C compilers. The Occam HLL is available to be used on the transputers.

References 1. C. L. Seitz, "The Cosmic Cube," *Comm. ACM*, Vol. 28, No. 1, pp. 22–23, Jan. 1985.

2. J. P. Hayes, T. Mudge, Q. F. Stout, S. Colley, J. Palmer, "A Microprocessor-based Hypercube Supercomputer," *IEEE MICRO*, Vol. 6, No. 5, pp. 6–17, Oct. 1986.

3. J. P. Hayes, *Computer Architecture and Organization*, 2nd. ed., McGraw-Hill, NY, 1988, Chapter 7.

4. P. Wiley, "A Parallel Architecture Comes of Age at Last," *IEEE Spectrum*, June 1987, pp. 46–50.

5. N. Mokhoff, ''Parallelism Breeds a New Class of Supercomputers,'' *Computer Design*, March 15, 1987, pp. 53–64.

6. N. Mokhoff, ''Hypercube Architecture Leads the Way for Commercial Supercomputers in Scientific Applications,'' *Computer Design*, May 1, 1986, pp. 28–30.

7. J. Bond, ''Parallel-processing Concepts Finally Come Together in Real Systems,'' *Computer Design*, June 1, 1987, pp. 51–74.

8. R. Asbury, S. G. Frison, T. Roth, ''Concurrent Computers Ideal for Inherently Parallel Problems,'' *Computer Design*, Sept. 1, 1985, pp. 99–107.

9. ''iPSC/2,'' *Intel Document Order No. 280110–001*, 1988.

10. S. P. Morse, E. J. Isaacson, D. J. Albert, *The 80386/387 Architecture*, John Wiley and Sons, NY, 1987.

11. S. Hawkinson, *The FPS T-Series: A Parallel Vector Supercomputer*, FPS Inc., Portland, OR, Nov. 13, 1986.

12. K. A. Frenkel, ''Evaluating Two Massively Parallel Machines,'' *Comm. ACM*, Vol. 19, No. 8, pp. 752–758, Aug. 1986.

CHAPTER 10

Switch Network Systems

10.1 The BBN Butterfly

The BBN Advanced Computers, Inc. Butterfly system contains up to 256 *processor nodes* [1–7]. This 256 figure is theoretical. In practice, only 128 processors are currently implemented.

Each processor node contains:

1. MC 68020 CPU, 16.67MHz, 2.5 MIPS performance.
2. MC 68882 Floating Point coprocessor.
3. MC 68851 *Paged Memory Management Unit* (PMMU).
4. Bit-sliced, microcoded (32 KByte Control Store), AMD2901 coprocessor, called *Processor Node Controller* (PNC). It manages memory and includes extensions to the instruction set to support multiprocessing.
5. Up to four MBytes of main memory (RAM) and 128 MBytes PROM.

FIGURE 10.1. Processor node block diagram (courtesy of BBN Advanced Computers, Inc.).

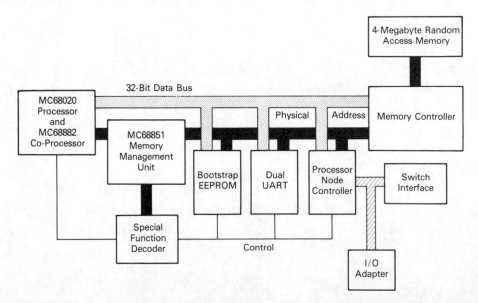

6. I/O bus adapter, interface to the Butterfly switch, and dual-channel RS-232 serial
   port for diagnostics. (see Figure 10.1)

All main memories of all nodes form a pool of *shared memory*, directly accessible by
all processors through the system's logarithmic, packet-switched communication network,
the *Butterfly Switch*. An average access time to another node's memory is four micro-
seconds. The switch bandwidth is 32 MBits/sec. per path. The basic Butterfly Switch
structure was introduced in Chapter 2 and illustrated in Figures 2.9 and 2.10. A general
memory-processor interconnection (16 nodes) is shown in Figure 10.2. A more specific
16-input/16-output system with a message transition example is illustrated in Figure
10.3. The destination is determined by the 1110 encoding; the least significant 10 for
the first stage and the most significant 11 for the second stage. A 64-processor interconnection is given in Figure 10.4.

FIGURE 10.2. Processor nodes and switch for a 16 processor configuration
(courtesy of BBN Advanced Computers, Inc.)

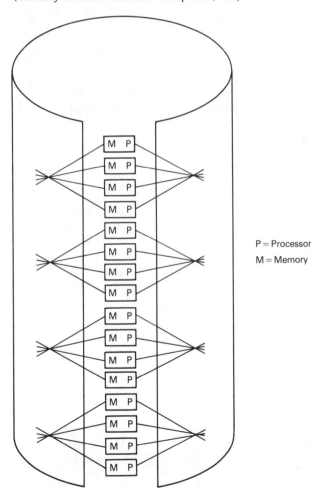

P = Processor
M = Memory

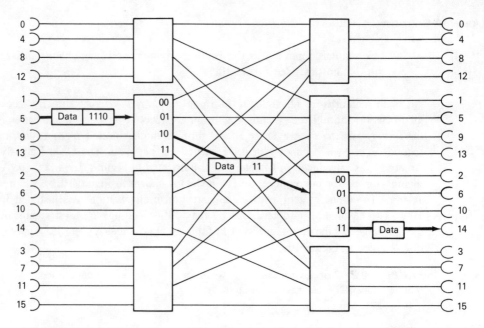

FIGURE 10.3. A packet in transit through a butterfly switch (courtesy of BBN Advanced Computers Inc.).

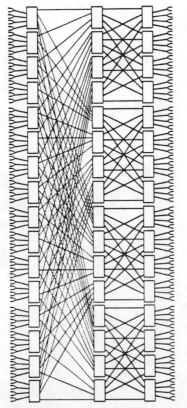

FIGURE 10.4. Switch for a 64 processor butterfly system (courtesy of BBN Advanced Computers Inc.).

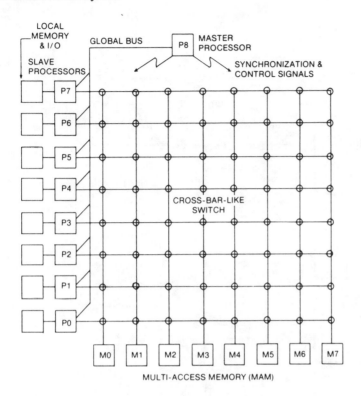

The interconnection switch allows simultaneous reads and writes of the global multi-access memory without multiplexing

FIGURE 10.5. The IP-1 system (courtesy of IPM, Inc.).

At the heart of the Butterfly Switch Network are custom VLSI chips called switching nodes. Each node is made up of eight finite state machines clustered around a crossbar network. A switch node examines a packet which enters one of its four left-side input channels, and routes the packet to the appropriate output port as determined by the first two bits of the packet's destination address. After the first bits are discarded, the remaining bits are passed to the next node. This process continues until the packet has reached the designated processor node. The switch provides a path from every processor node to every other. It is designed so that a packet encounters the same number of routing steps and arrives at any destination regardless of where it enters the network.

The Butterfly Switch does not have a dedicated path between processor nodes. As a result, two messages could arrive at the same switching node and require the same output port. In this case, one message proceeds and the other retreats until later retransmission. It is important to note that a single switching node can concurrently manage up to four messages that do not require the same output port.

BBN currently markets the Butterfly GP1000 system. The Butterfly GP1000 implements and Mach1000 OS, developed at Carnegie-Mellon University and ported to BBN. (See previous discussion in Chapter 4, subsection 4.5.3.) The Mach was found particularly

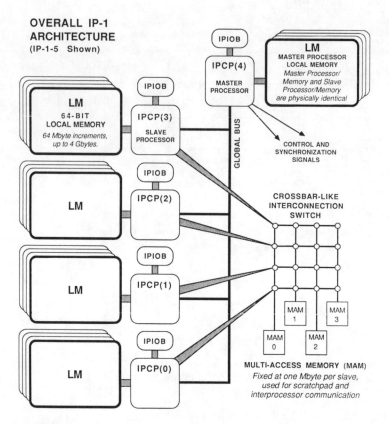

OVERALL IP-1
ARCHITECTURE
(IP-1-5 Shown)

IPIOB

IPCP(4)
MASTER
PROCESSOR

LM
MASTER PROCESSOR
LOCAL MEMORY
*Master Processor/
Memory and Slave
Processor/Memory
are physically identical*

LM
64-BIT
LOCAL MEMORY
*64 Mbyte increments,
up to 4 Gbytes.*

IPIOB

IPCP(3)
SLAVE
PROCESSOR

GLOBAL BUS

CONTROL AND
SYNCHRONIZATION
SIGNALS

LM

IPIOB

IPCP(2)

CROSSBAR-LIKE
INTERCONNECTION
SWITCH

LM

IPIOB

IPCP(1)

MAM 1   MAM 3

MAM 0   MAM 2

LM

IPIOB

IPCP(0)

MULTI-ACCESS MEMORY (MAM)
*Fixed at one Mbyte per slave,
used for scratchpad and
interprocessor communication*

IPIOB = INTERNATIONAL PARALLEL INPUT/ OUTPUT BOARD

IPCP(n) = INTERNATIONAL PARALLEL 64-BIT CPU BOARD
8 or 16 Mbytes onboard. **CPU CAN PHYSICALLY ADDRESS 256 TBYTES.**

FIGURE 10.6. IP-1 architecture (courtesy of IPM, Inc.).

suitable for multiprocessing operation when supported by the Butterfly hardware design. In addition to C and FORTRAN, the GP1000 supports GP-Scheme (a dialect of Lisp) and GP-Lisp languages. It also features a special real-time OS, called pSOS, developed by Software Components, Inc. The pSOS currently operates in numerous embedded systems for signal processing, real time scheduling, machine vision, real-time simulation and data communication.

Future plans include switching from the MC68020 as an individual processor to the RISC-type M88000 family. The overall performance is expected to increase by an order of magnitude; a factor of about eight for integer, and about 20 for floating point operations. The new system is called TC2000.

10.2 The IP-1 Crossbar System

About the only commercial multiprocessor, which uses a crossbar interconnection switch between the CPUs and the main memory, is the IP-1 [8], manufactured by International Parallel Machines, Inc. The 8 × 8 switch connects eight proprietary, 64-bit processors to eight memory modules, organized as a multiport, *Multi-Access Memory* (MAM). A ninth processor acts as an overall system manager (the master processor). Among other things, it configures the switch network and synchronizes the eight slave processors. Each processor (IPCP) has its own local memory of up to four GBytes (in addition to

FIGURE 10.7. The IPCP processor (courtesy of IPM, Inc.).

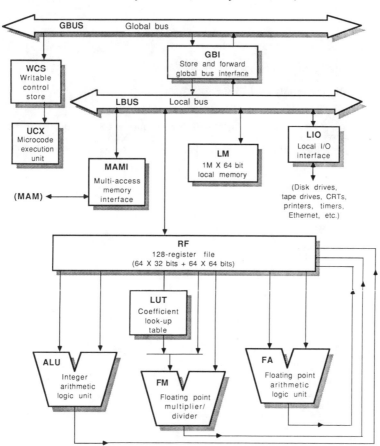

the shared MAM) and a parallel and serial I/O port. The IP-1 system is illustrated in Figures 10.5 and 10.6 and in the IPCP diagram in Figure 10.7.

The top configuration main memory is 1024 MBytes with a top performance of 80 MIPS. The IP-1 has a very high performance over price figure (see Chapter 13).

The OS is a proprietary IPOS, particularly designed to support multi-user parallel processing. An optional Unix System V front end is supported. The HLLs currently offered are C and FORTRAN.

References   1. *Butterfly Products Overview*, BBN Advanced Computers, Inc., Oct. 14, 1987.

2. W. Crowther et al., "The Butterfly Parallel Processor," *Comp. Arch. Tech. Comm. Newsletter*, IEEE Comp. Society, Sept./Dec. 1985, pp. 18–45.

3. G. E. Schmidt, "The Butterfly Parallel Processor," *Proc. 2nd. Int. Conf. on Supercomputers*, *ICS 87*, Vol. I, pp. 362–365, Santa Clara, CA, May 4–8, 1987.

4. K. Marrin, "Packet-switched Communications Extend Multiprocessor's Range," *Computer Design*, Sept. 1, 1986, pp. 20–23.

5. "Butterfly Parallel Processor Overview," *BBN Report No. 6148*, March 6, 1986.

6. C. D. Howe, B. Moxon, "How to Program Parallel Processors," *IEEE Spectrum*, Sept. 1987, pp. 36–41.

7. *Butterfly GP1000 Overview*, BBN Advanced Computers Inc., Nov. 10, 1988.

8. R. Chang, "Parallel Processing Computer Overcomes Memory Contention," *Computer Design*, Sept. 15, 1985, pp. 113–116.

CHAPTER 11

Multiprocessing Capabilities of Microprocessors

11.1 Introductory Comments

As argued earlier, the fast and widespread manufacturing and use of powerful and low-cost multiprocessors is due to the development of VLSI chips, particularly in high-performance microprocessors. In fact, a significant number of commercial multiprocessors uses off-the-shelf microprocessor CPU chips as individual processors of the system. These multiprocessors can actually be called *multimicroprocessors*. The Motorola MC68020 is used as a CPU in the BBN Butterfly (section 10.1), Flexible Compute Co. Flex/32, Arete Systems Corp Series 1000, EnMass Computer Corp. E/CS, Mass Comp. Corp. MC5000 [1,2]. The MC68020 is used as the IP in the Alliant, and Alliant's CE features the MC68020 architecture (see Chapter 7). The Intel 80286 is used in the iPSC and the 80386 is used in the iPSC/2 (section 9.2). The 80386 is also used as the CPU in the Sequent Symmetry system (section 8.2). The National Semiconductor NS32032 and NS32332 are used in the Encore Multimax (section 8.3), the NS32032 is used in the Sequent Balance (section 8.4). Undoubtedly the above and newly developed microprocessors will continue to be used as CPUs in multiprocessors.

The microprocessors manufacturers have anticipated this trend and have included a number of multiprocessor features such as atomic (uninterruptible and indivisible) semaphore handling instructions (see Chapter 3), bus arbitration facilities, and cache coherence policies in their basic design. It is the purpose of the following sections to survey the above features for some major microprocessor manufacturers (such as Motorola, Intel and National Semiconductors) whose products have already been used and most probably will continue to be used in the realization of multiprocessors.

11.2 Motorola MC68020, MC68030, and M88000

The MC68020 [3] chip is the first full-fledged 32-bit microprocessor manufactured by Motorola. It has been inherently predesigned for multiprocessor implementation [4] and it was already used in this capacity by a number of manufacturers, as we just discussed. The basic multiprocessor-oriented features, offered by the MC68020 are:

(a) Semaphore support with atomic (indivisible) instructions (see Chapter 3).

(b) Bus-sharing control signals to be used by a number of processors and connected to the same bus.

Some authors [4] count the MC68020 coprocessor interface, hardware-supported facilities as multiprocessor support features. The coprocessor, although capable of high-speed processing (particularly of floating point computation) concurrent with the 68020 CPU, despite the endowment of its own instruction set, *is not* a processor capable of standing alone "on its own feet." It can not function without the 68020 CPU, however the 68020 can function without the coprocessor. Therefore, the Motorola coprocessor (such as the MC68881, MC68882 Floating Point units, or the MC68851 *Paged Memory Management Unit* (PMMU) *is not* a processor of comparable capabilities to the MC68020 CPU. Thus, an MC68020 tightly coupled with one or more of the above coprocessors, is not a multiprocessor by Enslow's definition accepted in this text (see Chapter 1). It can be considered as a processor with an *attached processor*. A more powerful processing system than a stand-alone CPU, but still not a multiprocessor.

The simplest semaphore handling instruction of the 68020 is the *Test And Set*:

TAS ea; where ea = effective address.

The ea may be specified by any data alterable addressing mode of the 68020. It was also offered in the preceding 16-bit products of Motorola (the 68000, and the 68010). The TAS instruction is executed in an indivisible *read-modify-write* (RMW) bus cycle that locks other processors out of a multiport memory during a semaphore operation (see section 3.3). When the execution of TAS starts, the processor reads a byte from memory (the semaphore, specified by ea) and checks the operand, setting the condition codes accordingly. Then it writes the operand back to the same address with the most significant bit *set*, regardless of its previous state. An external control pin RMC^* (low asserted) is activated during the entire operation, to let the external logic know that an atomic RMW bus cycle is in progress. In this way, the indivisibility of the above instruction is supported by the hardware [4].

In some systems it may be necessary to perform operations more complicated than testing and setting on the semaphores. It may be inefficient to lock a system variable with a semaphore, modify it, and then unlock it. To reduce the amount of memory overhead required for individual semaphores, the MC68020 implements two special instructions, namely, *Compare And Swap* (CAS) and CAS2 which were not previously available on earlier products. These instructions utilize the same indivisible RMW bus cycle as the TAS, but they perform more complex operations that are tailored to the manipulation of counters, stack, and queue pointers. The two instructions operate on sets of three operands and execute a compare to, and an optional update of the system variable. Two of the above operands are in the 68020 Data Registers, Di (i = 0, 1, . . . , 7) and one is in memory, specified by an effective address (ea). (Any 68020 alterable memory addressing mode can be used.) The Compare And Swap instruction works as follows:

CAS.X   Dc, Du, ea

where X indicates the operand size: X = size
B = Byte (8 bits)
W = Word (16 bits)
L = Longword (32 bits)

The operation proceeds in the following steps:

1. Read the operand (byte, word, or longword as defined by X) at the memory location, defined by ea, and compare it to the value in the *compare register* (Dc).
2. If (ea) = (Dc), then write the value contained in the *update register*, Du, to the memory location, defined by ea, achieving (ea) = (Du).
3. If (ea) ≠ (Dc), then load the operand value, (ea) into Dc, achieving (Dc) = (ea).

The following example, illustrates the use of the CAS instruction to update a system counter [4]. Assume that a variable SYSCNT (a word of 16-bit size) resides in the shared memory and is used as a counter for the number of times that a certain event has happened in the system. Any processor in the system may perform this event, and thus update the counter. The update procedure should not be interruptible. The following loop guarantees that the variable is properly updated:

```
        MOVE.W   SYSCNT, D0   ;   load SYSCNT into D0
LOOP    MOVE.W   D0,D1        ;   move (D) into D1
        ADDQ.W   #1,D1        ;   increment D1 by 1
        CAS.W    D0,D1,SYSCNT;   D0=Dc, D1=Du
                             ;   SYSCNT = ea
        BNE      LOOP         ;   Branch if not equal to LOOP
                             ;   Branch if Z = 0, or if previous result not
                             ;   a zero
                             ;   In other words, if (D0) ≠ SYSCNT
                             ;   Z is the zero flag.
```

When this loop is entered, the program first reads the old value of the counter (D0), makes a copy of it (into D1), and then increments the copy (D1, the update register). Then the CAS instruction is used to read the counter again, and if it has not been changed by another task since the first read (SYSCNT = D0), then the incremented value (in D1) is written to memory (into SYSCNT) and the counter update is complete. If another task in the system had updated the counter since this task read it (SYSCNT ≠ D0), then the compare will fail, the new value (in SYSCNT) is copied to D0, the conditional branch is taken, and another attempt is made to update the counter. If the CAS instruction were not available, the program would use a similar loop with the TAS instruction to lock a semaphore associated with the SYSCNT location. When ownership of the counter was obtained, the update operation would be executed, followed by an unlock operation. Thus, CAS provides a more efficient mechanism for manipulating shared critical structures (see section 3.3).

The CAS2 instruction operates similarly to CAS, but it uses two sets of three operands, performing two comparisons and two settings with the same atomic instruction. Both comparisons must succeed in order for the memory to be updated. Its operands can be words or longwords only [3,4].

The Motorola MC68030, an upgraded version of the 68020, contains all of the features discussed above [5–7]. It does have some additional multiprocessor-related features. The 68020 had an instruction cache of 256 bytes on chip. Since the instruction cache is not written into, there was no potential problem of cache coherency (see Chapter 5). The 68030 has both an instruction and a data cache on chip of 256 bytes each. A cache coherency problem may arise in a 68030-based multiprocessor, since the data cache can be written into and modified. This possibility has been taken into account by the MC68030 designers.

The MC68030 Data Cache has two write policies:

1. *No-write allocate*. When the CPU performs a write to memory (store) operation, if there is a Data Cache:

    (a) *Hit*, the entry in the cache and the corresponding memory location (a *write through* policy is implemented) are updated;

    (b) *Miss*, the memory location is updated; there is no change in the cache.

2. *Write-allocate*. CPU write operation as above,

    (a) *Hit*, both memory and cache updated;

    (b) *Miss*, memory updated, cache updated if the written entry is a longword (32 bits) on a longword address (divisible by four) boundary, else the entry is invalidated.

The write allocate policy is useful in the case of *dual-sourced addresses*. That is, if two separate tasks use the same physical location (a shared location) to write into, stale data may be generated if the no-write-allocate policy is adopted. However, the write-allocate policy assures that the same new entry will appear in both the data cache and the memory immediately upon the completion of the write operation. This tends to support memory coherence (see Chapter 5). The 68030 OS (the supervisor mode) can switch between the two policies just by setting (for write-allocate) or clearing (for no-write-allocate) a bit in the Cache Control Register in the CPU.

Using the Cache Control Register the OS can invalidate any entry in the cache. This permits the implementation of the Cache Flush policy of cache coherence (see Chapter 5) in a 68030-based system. The implementation of Cache Flush will be particularly enhanced by the fact that the 68030 uses the write-through policy.

There are a number of hardware control lines which can be used in the implementation of various cache coherence policies, particularly those which use the notion of non-cacheable data. The external CDIS* signal disables the cache. The external CIIN* signal allows an external device to inhibit the caching of data that for any reason is non-cacheable. The internal signal CIOUT* indicates that the 68030 is accessing information that should not be cached. It can be used to enable or disable additional external cache. Cacheability of data is determined by the on-chip memory management system.

Motorola has recently announced a new microprocessor family M88000, completely unrelated to the M68000 products [8]. The M88000 belongs to the category of *Reduced Instruction Set Computers* (RISC) [9], a popular trend in the computer industry. The 88000 family currently features two chips:

1, MC88100 32-bit RISC CPU with 51 instructions, 32 (32-bit) general purpose registers, on-chip IEEE standard single- and double-precision floating point operation, separate 32-bit Data Address, Data, Instruction buses and a 30-bit instruction address bus.

2. MC88200 *Cache Memory Management Unit* (CMMU), featuring a 16 KByte, four-way set-associative data or instruction cache. Up to eight CMMU chips can be configured with a single 88100 for a 128 KByte cache.

The MC88100 CPU features an indivisible *exchange register with memory* (xmem) instruction for semaphore testing and multiprocessor synchronization. The MC88200 provides the capability to monitor the memory bus transactions of other devices in order to provide cache coherency in a multiprocessing environment. When the MC88200 is not the bus master, it optionally monitors all global transactions of other bus masters to ensure that cached data remains consistent with main memory. When a device, connected to the memory bus, accesses information that is resident in the MC88200 cache, the MC88200 preempts the access and updates its cache or main memory as appropriate to ensure data consistency.

A multiprocessor, consisting of up to four MC88100 CPUs and up to eight MC88200 CMMUs, called *HYPERmodule*, has been announced by Motorola [10]. Its expected performance at 20 MHZ is up to 50 MIPS, 20 MFLOPS or 100,000 dhrystones. It is a bus-oriented system.

11.3   Intel 80386

The 80386 is the first commercial 32-bit microprocessor manufactured by Intel [11–18]. The previously announced and later withdrawn 432 system, should be considered as an experimental product. As mentioned in section 11.1, it is used in the Sequent Symmetry (section 8.2) and in the Intel iPSC/2 (section 9.2). The 80386 has a number of multiprocessor-support features.

The 80386 has a semaphore handling instruction

XCHG Reg, EA

where Reg is a byte, or word (16 bit), or doubleword (32 bit) operand, residing in one of the CPU general purpose registers, and EA is an effective address (in a CPU register or in memory), using any of the 80386 addressing modes [15]. The instruction accomplishes the following:

1. The contents of Reg and EA are exchanged.

2. All flags are affected.

3. The CPU asserts a control pin LOCK*, which helps to ensure the indivisibility of the XCHG instruction, by transmitting a locking signal to the external logic.

For instance, the EA can represent a semaphore, located in memory at the address SMPH (symbolic representation). The CPU attempts to test and set the semaphore SMPH in the following manner [11]:

```
      MOV AL, 1      ; transfer the value 1 into the 8-bit register AL
LI:  XCHG AL, SMPH; SMPH <-----> AL
      CMP AL, 0      ; (AL)=0?, if yes, setting completed
      JNE LI         ; if not, try again at LI
      ; continue execution of the critical section if (SMPH)
      ; was zero before the test and now it has been set
      ; to prevent another processor from entering the same
      ; critical section (see section 3.3)
```

The XCHG instruction is similar to the Motorola TAS instruction (section 11.2).

The LOCK* signal can be set also for other instructions, such as bit change and test, one and two operand arithmetic and logic instructions. To accomplish this the user has to place the word LOCK in front of the assembly opcode mnemonic. The assembler will place a LOCK prefix byte in front of the machine language encoding of the instruction. The system hardware will assert the LOCK* control signal during the execution of the prefixed instruction. The LOCK* signal can lock access to any part of the memory with the help of the appropriate logic circuitry. There are five instances when the 80386 issues a LOCK* signal [13]:

1. Automatically when executing the XCHG instruction, even without a prefix.

2. While loading segment descriptors in order to prevent their modification while being transferred.

3. While acknowledging interrupts in order to keep other data off the bus.

4. While setting the busy bit of a *Task State Segment* (TSS) descriptor in order to keep two different processors from switching to the same task.

5. While updating page table entries.

All of the above events are supportive of multiprocessing operations.

The 80386 is endowed with a very efficient task switching, hardware and software supported, mechanism [11–18]. There is a task switch instruction which provides the OS with the ability to rapidly switch between tasks or processes. The task switch operation performs the following:

(a) Saves the entire state (context) of the interrupted task, including all CPU registers in a data structure called *Task State Segment* (TSS), pointed to by *TSS Register* (TSSR). The TSS is stored in the memory and the TSSR is a CPU control register.

(b) Loads a new execution state of the interrupting task, to be executed. The TSSR is loaded with new data pointing to the new TSS. CPU registers are loaded from the new TSS.

(c) Performs protection checks.

(d) Commences execution of the new task.

The task switch is invoked by an intersegment jump or call instruction, which refers a specific TSS. It may also be invoked by an interrupt. There is a field within the TSS which points to the next task in line (the next TSS) in a linked task chain.

It can of course be argued that the above mechanism supports multitasking in a uniprocessor, however, it definitely supports multiprocessing operation as well.

The 80386 does not have an on-chip cache. However, Intel manufactures an auxiliary Cache Controller chip, the 82385, designed to work in an 80386-based system with an external cache [12]. The 82385 can control an instruction and/or data cache of up to 32 KBytes. A write-through policy of immediate main memory update is supported. The 82385 implements a bus watching procedure to maintain cache coherence (see Chapter 5). When the 82385 cache controller intercepts a write operation that will modify a main memory location that is also in the cache, it invalidates the cache stale copy. This forces the updated memory location to be reloaded into the cache and prevents the cache from yielding old information. The 82385 also maintains cache coherency with respect to I/O (see Chapter 5) by watching multiple device DMAs via the system bus. For systems that support a dual ported memory structure, where bus watching cannot detect main memory changes, the 82385 provides a cache flush option. The cache controller also supports a hardware cache flush for use in diagnostic routing.

11.4 National Semiconductor NS32532

The National Semiconductor Series 32000 microprocessor family [19] features 32-bit microprocessors such as NS32032, NS32332, and NS32532. As mentioned in section 11.1, the NS32032, NS32332, and the NS32532 were used in the Encore Multimax products (section 8.3).

The 32000 architecture provides a semaphore handling instruction, *Set Bit Interlocked*, (SBITI) which sets the register or memory bit operand to one, while affecting the flags. In addition, the CPU Interlocked Operation output pin is activated to interlock accesses to the semaphore, while the SBITI instruction is executed. This feature is similar to the TAS operation on MC68020 or MC68030 (section 11.2) and the XCHG on the 80386 (section 11.3).

The NS32032 and the NS32332 do not have an on-chip cache. The NS32532 does have an on-chip 512 Byte instruction cache and an one KByte data cache. Thus, the problem of cache coherence may arise in a 32532-based multiprocessor. The NS32532 provides several mechanisms for maintaining coherence between the on-chip data caches and external memory [20].

In software, the use of caches can be inhibited for individual pages by appropriately encoding a bit in page table entries. There is a CINV (cache invalidate) instruction which can be executed to invalidate entirely the instruction and/or data cache. The CINV instruction can also be used to invalidate a single 16-bit block in either or both caches.

In hardware, the use of caches can be inhibited for individual locations using the CIIN input control signal. A cache invalidation request can cause the entire instruction and/or data cache to be invalidated. A cache invalidation request can also cause invalidation of a single set in either or both caches. The cache invalidation mechanisms are useful in implementing cache coherence policies, involving the declaration of non-cacheable information or cache flush (see Chapter 5).

The CPU provides all the necessary information on the system interface to permit the addition of an external bus watching mechanism to maintain cache coherence.

References 1. D. Simpson, "Multiprocessors Use Radical Architectures," *Mini–Micro Systems*, May 1986, pp. 77–88.

2. J. Bond, "Parallel Processing Concepts Finally Come Together in Real Systems," *Computer Design*, June 1, 1987, pp. 51–74.

3. *MC68020 32-Bit Microprocessor User's Manual*, 2nd. ed., Prentice-Hall, Englewood Cliffs, NJ, 1985.

4. B. Beims, "Multiprocessing Capabilities of the MC68020 32-Bit Microprocessors," *Motorola Document AR220*, WESCON 1984.

5. *MC68030 Enhanced 32-Bit Microprocessor User's Manual*, 2nd. ed., Prentice-Hall, Englewood Cliffs, NJ, 1988.

6. D. Lieberman, "The 68030 Microprocessor: A Window on 1988 Computing," *Computer Design*, Jan. 1, 1988, pp. 20–23.

7. "MC68030 Technical Summary," *Motorola Document BR508/D*, 1986.

8. R. Wilson, "Motorola Unveils New RISC Microprocessor Flagship," *Computer Design*, May 1, 1988, pp. 21–24.

9. D. Tabak, *RISC Architecture*, RSP, U.K., and John Wiley and Sons, NY, 1987.

10. "HYPERMODULE—A New Dimension in RISC Technology," *Motorola Document BR 619/D*, 1988.

11. S. P. Morse, E. J. Isaacson, D. J. Albert, *The 80386/387 Architecture*, John Wiley and Sons, NY, 1987.

12. C. H. Pappas, W. H. Murray, III, *80386 Microprocessor Handbook*, Osborne/McGraw-Hill, Berkeley, CA, 1988.

13. P. Brumm, D. Brumm, *80386 A Programming and Design Handbook*, TAB Books, Blue Ridge Summit, PA, 1987.

14. *80386 Hardware Reference Manual*, Intel o.n. 231732–001, 1986.

15. *80386 Programmer's Reference Manual*, Intel o.n. 230985–001, 1986.

16. *80386 System Software Writer's Guide*, Intel o.n. 231499–001, 1987.

17. K.A.El-Ayat, R. K. Agarwal, "The Intel 80386—Architecture and Implementation," *IEEE Micro*, Vol. 5, No. 6, pp. 4–22, Dec. 1985.

18. D. Tabak, "The Intel 80386 and New 32-bit Microprocessors," *Microprocessing and Microprogramming*, Vol. 19, No. 1, pp. 59–74, Jan. 1987.

19. C. Hunter, *Series 32000 Programmer's Reference Manual*, Prentice-Hall, Englewood Cliffs, NJ, 1987.

20. "NS32532 High-performance 32-Bit Microprocessor," *National Semiconductor Document RRD-B20M107*, Oct. 1987.

21. D. Alpert, J. Levy, B. Maytal, *Architecture of the NS32532 Microprocessor*, ICCD, NY, Oct. 5–8, 1987.

PART THREE

SYSTEM EVALUATION AND IMPLEMENTATION

CHAPTER 12

Realization of Multiprocessor Design Problems in Actual Systems

12.1 Introductory Comments

Some problems, involved in the design of multiprocessors, such as synchronization, scheduling, memory latency, *hot spots*, memory coherence, software and OS, have been discussed in Part One, particularly in Chapter 5. Examples of a number of approaches to cope with the above problems can be found in part two, where several commercial multiprocessors are surveyed. It is the purpose of this chapter to concentrate on the following question: how are the multiprocessor design problems, discussed earlier, actually solved in various multiprocessing systems, which have been developed and designed? How is the solution realized? The discussion in the following sections will deal with the following problems:

- Synchronization and Scheduling;
- Memory Latency (including the *hot spots* problem);
- Memory Coherence; and
- Software.

Since Chapter 4 has been particularly dedicated to multiprocessor OS, including examples of actual systems, the topic will not be repeated here. There may be some repetition of details, mentioned in earlier chapters (particularly in Part Two), however it was felt that a concentrated presentation of the realization of some multiprocessor design issues, in real-life systems, will be of interest and use to the reader. Design solutions in both experimental prototypes and commercial multiprocessors will be presented. Although an experimental prototype may exist in only a single installation, may never be reproduced, and never be commercially implemented in its original form, its experience may have a crucial impact on systems designed and manufactured in the future. A number of experimental multiprocessor prototypes, such as the Carnegie-Mellon C.mmp[1], the NYU Ultracomputer [2, 12], the IBM RP3[3, 4, 12] and the University of Illinois CEDAR [5, 8–11] have served as guidelines to a number of industrial designs and other research endeavors. The above list of experimental systems, as well as the set of commercial systems described in Part Two, is certainly not complete; many more systems exist. It is impractical to attempt to cover all existing systems in a single text. However, it is felt that the covered systems constitute a fair representation of the current state of the art of multiprocessor design.

12.2 *Synchronization and Scheduling*

Almost all multiprocessor systems have atomic (indivisible) synchronization instructions for handling semaphores and other variables associated with critical sections in the shared memory (see section 3.3). One of the most popular synchronization instructions is the *Test And Set* (described in sections 3.3 and 11.2). The NYU Ultracomputer [2, 12] features a synchronization operation, the *Fetch And Add* (FAA), performed on an integer variable V and an integer expression e (see section 3.3). The atomic operation FAA fetches the old value of V and replaces it by the sum V + e. FAA can be further generalized to form the Fetch and f operation, where f(V,e) is a function (arithmetic or logical) on V and e. It is easy to check that the Test and Set on V is equivalent to a Fetch And OR on (V, TRUE), where OR is a logic or operation. The Ultracomputer implements the method of *barrier* synchronization [12] (described in section 3.2). The variable controlling the barrier is tested using the *Fetch And Add* instruction. This is helpful in enhancing the speedup when multiple processors reach the barrier together. Since Fetch And Add is implemented on the Ultracomputer at the memory, it takes no longer than an ordinary memory read and write (two memory cycles), and because the interconnection network is able to *combine* simultaneous Fetch And Adds (see section 12.3) accessing the same memory location, all processors can arrive at the barrier at the same time and receive an answer (one yes, the rest, no) in the same time required by one processor. In this way, the Ultracomputer designers avoid a potential bottleneck situation.

   The problem of synchronization is naturally connected to the problem of efficient interprocessor and processor-memory communication network. The RP3[3, 12], for instance, uses an Omega network (see Chapter 2) for interprocessor coordination.

   The synchronization of concurrent operations, running on different processors (CEs) of the Alliant, is performed by the *Concurrency Control Unit* (CCU) (see section 7.2). It features a 40-line *Concurrency Control Bus*, interconnecting all of the concurrently running processors, namely, the CEs. It is separate from the processor-memory dual bus, and it is specifically intended for transmitting synchronization information between the processors. The parallel processing synchronization is performed dynamically during execution. The synchronization operation of the CCU is supported by special *synchronization and concurrency control registers* (section 7.3) which contain data used in supervising concurrent execution (of iterative loops, for instance) of parts of a program on a number of CEs. The Alliant Unix-type OS, the Concentrix (section 7.4) has been specifically designed to handle dynamic scheduling of CE configurations.

   The University of Illinois CEDAR system [5, 8–10] is composed of a number of clusters, operating in parallel, as illustrated in Figure 12.2. Each cluster is a modified Alliant FX/8 system (see Chapter 7). The major modification done to the Alliant FX/8 to convert it into a Cedar cluster was to expand the crossbar switch between the CEs and the CE cache from 8 × 4 (see Figure 7.4) to an 8 × 8 crossbar switch (see Figure 12.2). The four additional ports are used to connect the CEs to a *Global Interface* (GI) which is the pathway to the *Global Switch* and to the *Global Memory Modules* (see Figure 12.2). The synchronization and scheduling within each cluster is naturally very similar to that on the Alliant. A *self-scheduling* procedure is adopted, where each CE having completed the execution of a specific loop iteration, requests the next unassigned

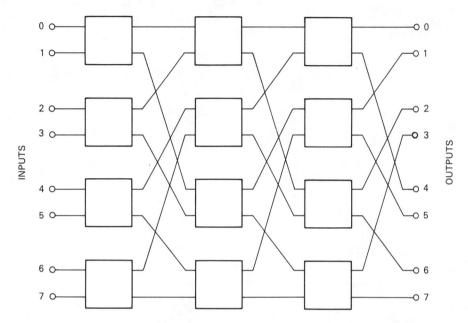

FIGURE 12.1. N=8 omega network

iteration from the concurrency control bus. The CE, completing the last iteration, proceeds to execute the instruction immediately after the parallel loop. Such an approach to parallelism, which avoids context switching, is called *microtasking*. An important characteristic of microtasking is that a parallel construct should execute independently of the number of processors available. Two types of *loop synchronization* schemes are used in this case:

1. Critical section locking; and
2. Cascade Synchronization, from lower iterations to higher ones, supported by the Alliant hardware.

For multiply-nested loops the Cedar system provides a higher level self-scheduling facility which allows each cluster to self-schedule an outer loop among the clusters. Within each cluster, microtasking can be applied to the inner loop nests.

The interprocess synchronization on the ELXSI (see section 8.1) is handled by a message-passing system, composed of links (transmitting the messages), and funnels (receiving the messages). This system, supported by both hardware and software, provides efficient intercommunication and synchronization of processes, running on different (or the same) processors.

The Sequent design (see section 8.2) provides each CPU with a *System Link and Interrupt Controller* (SLIC), which manages and coordinates multiple processors. All SLICs are connected by a bit-serial data line called the SLIC bus, for transmission of synchronizing information. The information, transmitted on the SLIC bus is in the form of command-response packets of fixed length.

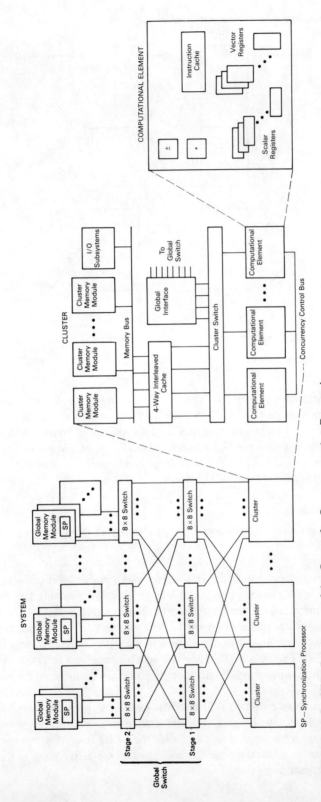

FIGURE 12.2. CEDAR (courtesy of the Center for Supercomputing Research and Development, University of Illinois).

132

The synchronization mechanism on the Encore Multimax (section 8.3) is provided by its UMAX OS. It provides support for semaphores, locks and a communication protocol, using the Annex. The Annex uses the Arpanet suite of communication protocols.

The hypercube-based systems, such as the NCUBE (section 9.1) and the iPSC (section 9.2), use message passing along serial communication lines for synchronization. The iPSC/2 carries a multitasking OS, called Node Executive/2(NX/2), which features round-robin scheduling in each node. The NX/2 is Unix-compatible, in particular with regard to files and I/O operations.

Of all the commercial systems surveyed, the Alliant hardware and software supported synchronization mechanism seems to be the most efficient. This is particularly evidenced in its 40-line concurrency control bus (as opposed to bit-serial lines on other systems) and its elaborate CCU with its special registers. The Omega network, implemented on the RP3 and the Ultracomputer, seems to be promising, however, it has not migrated to commercial systems as yet, apparently because of its higher cost, compared to a bus.

12.3   Memory Latency

The memory latency problem involves the minimization of access time between any processor and the memory (see Chapter 5). There are three basic approaches to cope with this problem, as implemented in actual multiprocessors:

1. To provide an efficient processor-memory communication network.
2. To provide a high hit ratio cache storage.
3. To provide each processor with a local memory.

Naturally, all approaches can be implemented in the same system.

The NYU Ultracomputer [2, 12] designers envisage a large scale multiprocessor, extendable to N = 4096 processors in the 1990s. A 64-processor prototype, using commercial microprocessors and memories is under development. The general Ultracomputer model features $N = 2**D$ processors and N memory modules. The memory latency problem naturally arises in any system with multiple processors and memory modules. The Ultracomputer primary approach to resolve the memory latency problem is by using an efficient processors-memory modules Omega-type (see Chapter 2) interconnection network. An example of an Omega network for N = 8 is shown in Figure 12.1. This network has the same topology as the rectangular SW banyan network of Goke and Lipovski [6]. The above N memory modules constitute the shared memory of the multiprocessor. The Ultracomputer Omega network has the following properties:

1. The network is *pipelined*, that is, the delay between messages equals the *switch cycle time* and not the network transit time, which grows logarithmically in N, since the total number of stages is $\log_2 N$ (see Chapter 2).
2. The network is *message switched*, that is, the switch settings are not maintained while a reply is awaited.

3. A queue is associated with each switch to enable concurrent processing of requests for the same port.

When concurrent loads and stores are directed at the same memory location and meet at a switch, they can be *combined* without introducing any delay by using the following procedure:

(a) *Load–Load*: Forward one of the two identical loads and satisfy each by returning the value obtained from memory.

(b) *Load–Store*: Forward the store and return its value to satisfy the load. This also takes care of using the latest update on a load to support coherence.

(c) *Store–Store*: Forward either store and ignore the other. An event when two processors attempt to store different values in the same memory location, simultaneously, may be a cause for memory incoherence. Such an event should be avoided.

Combining requests for memory access reduces communication traffic thus decreasing the lengths of switch queues, leading to lower network latency (that is, reduced memory access time). The combining of messages alleviates the *hot spots* problem of network messages congestion (see Chapter 5). A similar approach of message combining has also been adopted on the IBM RP3[3, 12].

Memory latency on the Ultracomputer is also reduced by equipping the processors with local cache memories and by interleaving memory addresses across the memory modules to distribute references and decrease congestion as much as possible.

The IBM experimental prototype, called the Research Parallel Processor Project, RP3[3, 4, 12], is a 512-processors system. It is composed of 512 *Processor-Memory Elements* (PMEs). Each PME is composed of an IBM ROMP processor [14, pp. 102–104], 32 KByte, two-way set associative (1024 lines/set, 16 bytes/line) cache, 4MBytes main memory, a floating point unit, and a memory management unit. Its expected full configuration performance is 1.3 GIPS (1300 MIPS), 800 MFLOPS, 13 GBytes/sec. interprocessor communication and 192 MBytes/sec I/O rate. The RP3 interconnection network is composed of two networks:

1. An *Omega* is a network containing 64-ports, six-stages, and 2×2 switches having the ability to *combine messages* (as in the Ultracomputer), in particular interprocessor coordination functions, directed to the same memory location.

2. A *low latency* rectangular SW banyan [6], similar to an Omega network, but providing dual source-sink paths. It has 128 ports and is constructed with four levels of 4×4 switches. The network provides dual paths between each source and sink. Two such dual path networks are actually used, one for requests (processors to memories), and one for replies (memories to processors). This both provides increased bandwidth, reduced latency and avoids the possibility of memory modules deadlock.

Both networks use a mixture of circuit and packet-switching where a message (read or write request) is pipelined across switch stages as if circuit-switched; but when blocked, some or all of the message is queued within a switch stage in a manner similar to packet-switching. Since messages are pipelined and complete paths need not be allocated or used, routing control can be localized at the switches, and throughput is robustly maintained with high traffic levels. All in all, a reduction of latency.

There are two other RP3 design features contributing to the reduction of memory latency:

(a) A wide-memory interleaving. The interleave amount is variable, set by a field in the mapping tables; and

(b) A movable boundary between local and global (shared) memory. Moving the boundary to one edge makes RP3 a pure local memory system. Moving the boundary to the other edge yields shared memory only. Intermediate boundary positions yield a "mixed mode," adjustable for efficient implementation and minimal latency, depending on the particular application. The above boundary is established as a part of the memory mapping mechanism.

The Cedar clusters (see Figure 12.2) [8] are connected to the Global Memory modules through a *packet-switching* (see Chapter 4), *Global Network* (GN), consisting of two unidirectional multiple-stage shuffle-exchange (see Chapter 2) networks. One goes from the clusters to the memories and the other, in the opposite direction. Each packet in the network can have up to four 64-bit words with the first word always an address/control word. The network consists of 8 × 8 crossbar switches, organized into two stages that are connected using the perfect shuffle scheme (see Chapter 2), with hardware queues at their entry ports. Each port is 80-bit wide: 64 bits of data, eight parity bits and four duplicated (for enhanced reliability) control signals which allow handshaking between network stages. The network has a cycle of 85 $nsec$ which provides a total bandwidth of 2.9 GBytes/sec. for a four-cluster 32-processor (4*8 CEs) Cedar system.

The Omega network appears to be an accepted means of reducing memory latency in research prototype multiprocessors. It may indeed turn out to be a superior solution, compared to others. However, its current high cost precludes its implementation in commercial systems. The only significant switching network, commercially implemented, is the 256-processor Butterfly Network (section 10.1). The announced Butterfly switch bandwith is 32 MBits/sec. per path.

Most commercial multiprocessors cope with the memory latency problem by providing a large cache. Practically each one has a *Translation Lookaside Buffer* (TLB) for caching mapping information from Virtual (Logical) to Physical (Real) addresses. The Alliant (see Chapter 7) features a cache composed of a number of blocks. Each cache block (quadrant) is accessible by all processors (CEs) through a crossbar interconnect network, (see Figure 7.4) whose bandwidth is 376 MBytes/sec. The total CE cache on the FX/8 is 128 KBytes, and the total ACE cache on the FX/80 is 512 KBytes. In addition, there is an 128 KByte IP cache on both systems. All of the above caches store instructions and data.

Other commercial multiprocessors feature cache storage separately for each CPU. The ELXSI CPU, (section 8.1) the 6460 has up to one MByte cache; 512 KByte instruction, 512 KByte data. For a maximal 10 6460s configuration, the total system cache is thus

10 MBytes. The Sequent Symmetry (section 8.2) features a 64 KByte cache (instructions and data) per CPU (80386). For a maximum of 30 CPUs configuration of the S81 system there is a total of 1.92 MByte storage. The Encore Multimax (section 8.3) features the same size of cache per CPU as the Sequent. The envisaged future Encore product Ultramax, will feature an Ultra Cache Card of up to 32 MBytes, accessible by all of the processors of a Multimax cluster (20 CPUs), as opposed to the currently implemented individual cache per CPU. Using a large cache, accessible by all processors, through an efficient network (as in the Alliant), constitutes a good and a relatively low cost solution (compared to the Omega network) to the memory latency problem.

12.4 Cache Coherence

The NYU Ultracomputer designers [2] originally proposed to use a *flush facility* (see Chapter 5) to maintain cache coherence. The flush facility enables the processor to force a write-back of cached shared values that have been modified. Basically, the Ultracomputer designers [13] favor a software solution using special instructions or system service calls, which explicitly alter the cacheability status of a data item, when issued during program execution. The RP3[3, 12] solves the cache coherence problem in software, by using the method of *noncachable shared* writable data (see Chapter 5). The noncachable information is marked as such by the compiler, in cooperation with the linker and run-time storage allocation system. The above non-cache marking is reflected in the memory map. A software solution has also been adopted in the CEDAR[11], where a compiler is used to generate cache management instructions to solve cache coherence problems.

The Alliant (see Chapter 7) features two basic approaches to enhance cache coherence (see Chapter 5):

(a) The *shared cache* approach (see Figure 7.4); and

(b) The "snoopy" *bus-watching* mechanism (see Figure 7.5).

It appears that the bus-watching ("snoopy") mechanism is also a popular feature predesigned on most modern 32-bit microprocessors (see Chapter 11).

The Sequent S system (section 8.2) implements a cache coherence mechanism similar to the cache flush (see Chapter 5) approach. The cache controller of the modifying processor broadcasts a message to all other processors that the modified data structure is no longer valid and a new copy (after a write-back) of it has to fetched from memory. If the data is needed urgently, before a write-back has been completed, it can be transferred directly from the modifier processor's cache.

A cache coherence management technique for hypercube multiprocessors (see Chapter 9) has been proposed by Emberson [7]. The only reasons for cache incoherence (see Chapter 5) in a hypercube system (a loosely coupled system) are:

1. *Process migration* from one processor to another; and

2. *Direct Memory Access* (DMA) from an I/O device.

The method proposed to cope with the above is of the cache flush type: cache entries invalidation by the OS when either DMA or process migration occurs. The cache invalidation mechanism is also supported by hardware by providing a special counter register called *counter tag*, managed by the OS and initialized to zero. As processes are created, the counter is incremented and the value of the counter is assigned to the process as its *cache tag*. To selectively invalidate the cache for a process, one increments the counter and assigns the process a new tag value by inserting the new tag into the cache tag register. Total cache flushes are only necessary when the counter wraps around. Although a complete hardware design has been provided [7], the actual implementation of the method in a real-life message-passing multiprocessor has not been announed (to the best of the author's knowledge).

12.5 Software

This section surveys some special software facilities and enhancements offered by some actual multiprocessor systems.

The Alliant (see Chapter 7) offers a special set of concurrency instructions in its assembly and machine language. These instructions are intended primarily for the compiler and OS writers. The average user would program in one of the HLLs (FORTRAN, C, Pascal, Ada) and may not be aware of this facility. Both the Alliant (see Chapter 7) and the Encore (section 8.3) offer parallelizing FORTRAN and Ada compilers.

The ELXSI system (section 8.1) features a software structure for virtual machine interface, called the *System Foundation*. It consists of 25 processes, offering the user four concurrent OS environments: EMBOS, EMS, AT&T Unix System V and Berkeley Unix 4.2 BSD (see section 8.1 for details). The ELXSI also provides a set of software tools called *system intrinsics* to aide in code parallelization.

The Encore Multimax (section 8.3) and the BBN Butterfly (section 10.1) feature the Mach OS, (subsection 4.5.3) specifically designed for multiprocessor implementation. The BBN also supports a special software methodology called the *Uniform System*. The Uniform System helps the users to manage the system resources, such as processors and memory modules. It manages processors by dynamically distributing computational tasks among them.

The CEDAR [5, 8–11] features a programming environment called *Faust*. It includes, in an integrated setting, editors, debuggers, compilers, an interactive restructurer, performance tools and computer graphics tools. The CEDAR OS is Xylem [10], based on the Alliant OS Concentrix (section 7.4), which is Unix-based. The Xylem particularly supports intercluster parallelism. An important feature in Xylem is the abstraction of a *process* consisting of a number of parallel *cluster tasks*. The Xylem notion of a process is much like that of Unix (see Chapter 4), essentially representing the entire state of execution of a program. However, it is the individual cluster tasks that execute (rather than the process), potentially on different physical clusters. Any cluster task of Xylem can create new cluster tasks, which become siblings of the creator, all belonging to the same process. Each cluster runs a copy of the same Xylem kernel, communicating primarily via data structures stored in global memory.

The CEDAR FORTRAN is an extension of the Alliant FX/FORTRAN (see section 7.5). It features constructs to express two types of loop parallelism:

1. *doall* (see Chapter 3) indicates that the iterations of the loop can be executed in parallel and that there is no restriction on the order in which these iterations may be scheduled for execution. There are two types of *doall* constructs:

   (a) *cdoall* uses the processors assigned to the cluster task to execute its iterations, and, if the number of processors is greater than one, uses the concurrency control hardware to start and schedule the loop. Expresses *intracluster parallelism*.

   (b) *sdoall* uses the processor complexes to execute each iteration. Expresses *intercluster parallelism*.

2. *doacross* (see Chapter 3), allows cascade synchronization on top of the critical section synchronization (section 12.2) allowed for *doalls*. Currently, CEDAR FORTRAN only allows *doacross* to be executed inside a cluster.

The BSD 4.3 UNIX has been extensively modified in the Ultracomputer project to provide an OS for the RP3[3, 12]. Most modifications (user invisible) consist of replacing many internal OS algorithms with serialization-free equivalents, such as enqueue/dequeue operations for scheduling[2]. While the system will do dynamic load balancing, a user will optionally be able to lock processes into processors to do application dependent static or dynamic load balancing. User-visible modifications include interprocess shared memory, load- and/or run-time use of distributed and local memory, and a *"spawn" primitive*, analogous to Unix' *"fork"* (see section 3.2), allowing simultaneous creation of many processes without having that operation cause a serial bottleneck. The CMU Unix-based Mach (see section 4.5.3) OS environment is provided on the RP3[12]. It was modified by NYU and IBM to eliminate internal serial sections and support highly parallel operation, using the combining synchronization primitives developed at NYU and supported on RP3. Unix seems to be a popular and almost exclusive OS in both commercial and research multiprocessor implementations. Notable exception is the EMS, emulating the VAX VMS, implemented as one of the four OS environments in the ELXSI (see section 8.1).

References 1. D. P. Siewiorek et al., "A Case Study of C.mmp, Cm*, and C.vmp, Parts I and II," *Proc. IEEE.* Vol. 66, No. 10, pp. 1178–1220, Oct. 1978.

2. A. Gottlieb et al., "The NYU Ultracomputer—Designing an MIMD Shared Memory Parallel Computer," *IEEE Trans. on Computers*, Vol. C-32, No. 2, pp. 175–189, Feb. 1983.

3. G. F. Pfister et al., "The IBM Research Parallel Processor Prototype (RP3): Introduction and Architecture," *Proc. 1985 Int. Conf. on Parallel Processing*, pp. 764–771, St. Charles, IL, Aug. 1985.

4. W. C. Brantley, K. P. McAuliffe, J. Weiss, "RP3 Processor-Memory Element," *Proc. 1985 Int. Conf. on Parallel Processing*, pp. 782–789, St. Charles, IL, Aug. 1985.

5. D. J. Kuck, E. S. Davidson, D. H. Lawrie, A. H. Lawrie, A. H. Sameh, "Parallel Supercomputing today and the Cedar Approach," Science, Vol. 231, pp. 967–974, Feb. 28, 1986.

6. L. R. Goke, G. J. Lipovsky, ''Banyan Networks for Partitioning Multiprocessor Systems,'' *Proc. 1st Annual Symp. On Computer Architecture*, pp. 21–28, 1973.

7. D. R. Emberson, ''Cache Coherence Management and Technique for Hypercube Multiprocessors,'' *Proc. 1987 Int. Conf. on Parallel Processing*, St. Charles, IL., Aug. 1987.

8. P. Emrath, D. Padua, P. C. Yew, ''Cedar Architecture and its Software,'' *Proc. 22nd Hawaii Int. Conf. System Science*, Vol. 1, pp. 306–315, Jan. 3–6, 1989.

9. D. A. Padua, ''The Cedar Parallel Processor: Machine Organization and Software,'' *Speedup*, Vol. 2, No. 1, pp. 26–31, Jan. 1988.

10. P. Emrath, ''Xylem: An Operating System for the Cedar Multiprocessor,'' *IEEE Software*, Vol. 2, No. 4, pp. 30–37, July 1985.

11. A. V. Veidenbaum, ''A Compiler-Assisted Cache Coherence Solution for Multiprocessors,'' *Proc. 1986 Int. Conf. on Parallel Processing*, pp. 1029–1035, St. Charles, IL, Aug. 1986.

12. G. S. Almasi, A. Gottlieb, *Highly Parallel Computing*, Benjamin/Cummings, Redwood City, CA, 1989.

13. A. Gottlieb, ''An Overview of the NYU Ultracomputer Project,'' *Ultracomputer Note #100*, NYU, April 1987.

14. D. Tabak, *RISC Architecture*, RSP, U.K. and John Wiley and Sons, NY, 1987.

CHAPTER 13

Comparison of Multiprocessor Systems

A summary of some basic properties of the systems presented in Part Two is given in Table 13.1. Wherever applicable, the data for the top product (maximal configuration) of a family have been listed. The data in Table 13.1 cannot be used directly for comparison purposes; it would be the same as comparing "apples to oranges." The design philosophy, configuration and implementation approaches of some of the systems are so different, that a direct comparison would be meaningless. It would make more sense to compare systems belonging to the same class of structure and with the same number of CPUs configured.

Let us take the bus-oriented systems (Alliant, Sequent, Encore, and ELXSI) separately, and the n-cube systems (NCUBE/10, Intel iPSC, FPS T-Series) separately. The BBN Butterfly will be grouped with the n-cube system. The IP-1 will not be compared since it is significantly different from the others.

The Alliant has only eight CPUs (the CEs), the combined FX/82 excepted, intended for actual multiprocessing (see Chapter 7). The 12 IPs are in the category of front-end hosts and IOPs. Therefore, an *eight-CPU* configuration for all bus-oriented systems will be taken, with the results shown in Table 13.2.

The ELXSI 6460 system, certainly takes the edge for integer processing (MIPS) and top physical main memory and cache configuration. It should be remembered, however, that the 6460 is a 64-bit machine, while all others are 32 bit. The Alliant is definitely superior for floating point computations.

In order to compare the n-cube systems, along with the Butterfly, an 128-node, seven-cube (maximal for iPSC) configuration is taken into account, as presented in Table 13.3. The table shows the overall storage, in MBytes for a 128-node system. The Transputer-based FPS T-Series has a significant edge for both floating point and integer performance. The iPSC/2 has the largest storage capability.

There is not much sense in comparing the two groups, listed above. One comment is in order though. While the bus-oriented systems are more universal-computing oriented, the n-cube systems, are geared for some very specific classes of problems, such as FFT for instance. For many classes of problems, the n-cube systems may be significantly underutilized, compared to the bus-oriented ones. Attempting to use the n-cubes as universal computing systems would result in considerable idle time for a significant percentage of their multiple CPUs.

Idle time may also be the lot of the bus-oriented systems, for some time periods, however, since much less CPUs, are involved, the problem is less serious. Generally speaking, there will be less idle time for a larger class of problems on the bus-oriented systems. On this point the Alliant seems to have an edge. A maximum of 12 IPs can be configured in the system. This could facilitate the continuous utilization of all processors

TABLE 13.1 Summary of system properties

System	Maximal Number of CPUs	CPU	Peak Performance MIPS	Peak Performance MFLOPS	Maximal Storage Main Memory MBytes	Maximal Storage Cache KBytes
Alliant FX/8	8 + 12*	custom (CE)	35	94	256	512
Alliant FX/80	8 + 12*	custom (ACE)	70	188	256	512
Alliant FX/82	16 + 24*	custom (ACE)	140	376	512	1024
Sequent B21	30	NS32032	21	2	28	240
Sequent S81	30	I80386	108	15	240	1920
Encore Multimax 520	20	NS32532	170	50	160	5120
ELXSI 6420	12	custom**	120	20	2048	768
ELXSI 6460	10	custom**	250	100	2048	10 MBytes
NCUBE/10	1024	custom	2048	512	512	—
Intel iPSC	128	I80286	100	8	64	—
Intel iPSC/2	128	I80386	512	141+	1024	—
FPS T-Series	16384	IMST414	114688	262000	16384	—
BBM Butterfly						
GP1000	256	MC68020	600	25	1024	—
IP–1	9	custom	80	160	1024	—

* IPs, MC68020; performance and cache data are for the CEs or ACEs only. Main memory is shared by all CEs and IPs.

** 64-bit CPU.

+ With the VX Vector option, 64 nodes, up to 1280 MFLOPS.

in a multi-user environment. The availability of a *dual* system bus and a separate concurrency bus, certainly enhances the overall system performance and utilization.

So far, Alliant and Encore have announced automatically parallelizing compilers for FORTRAN and Ada. In other systems, parallelization operations must be inserted by the user. However, other manufacturers have been reported to be working on automatic parallelization, to be offered in the future.

All of the systems offer a Unix-like, sometimes proprietary, sometime extended OS. The Alliant Concentrix OS, seems to be one of the best, currently available multiprocessor OS (see section 7.4), primarily by flexibly supporting concurrent operations over

TABLE 13.2 Comparison of an eight-CPU configuration of bus-oriented systems

System	MIPS	MFLOPS	Physical Main Memory MBytes	Cache KBytes
Alliant FX/80	70	188	256	512
Sequent B8	5.6	0.6	28	64
Sequent S27	28.8	4	80	512
Encore Mult. 520	68	20	160	512
ELXSI 6460	200	80 (32-bit)	2048	8 MBytes

TABLE 13.3. Comparison of a 128-processor
configuration of n-cube systems and the Butterfly.

System	MIPS	MFLOPS	MBytes
NCUBE/7	256	64	64
iPSC/2	512	141	1024
T-series (T/200)	896	1536	128
Butterfly GP1000	300	12	512

separate resources (CEs and IPs), and by supporting automatically parallelizing compilers.
On the other hand, one of the advantages of the ELXSI OS EMS (see section 8.1) is
that it is DEC VMS compatible. On the ELXSI system VMS system service calls are
supported without change, whereas they require editing to be used on the Alliant system
[1]. This is an important point in view of the wide spread of VAX systems among
numerous users. BBN and Encore have recently ported a high-quality Multiprocessor
OS, the Mach (see subsection 4.5.3), developed at the Carnegie Mellon University.
The Mach is a Unix extension.

The commercial multiprocessors, described in part two, have been compared by
their specifications and properties, announced by their manufacturers. A better way of
comparison between different computing systems is by monitoring their actual performance
in solving different problems. This can be done by running a number of selected benchmark
programs on the systems being compared, and noting the execution time, which can
sometimes also be expressed in terms of jobs per unit time.

The cost of the system is no less important than its speed. If systems A and B
accomplish the same task in about equal time, but system B costs twice as much as A,
then system A has a very definite advantage. Therefore, when comparing different systems,
it also makes sense to present data expressing the ratio of speed or throughput over
cost (speed/dollars).

A number of manufacturers have indeed conducted some benchmark studies, noting
the throughput and speed of performance, while comparing a number of different systems.
The relative cost of the compared systems has also been noted. The results of some of
these studies will be presented in the following paragraphs.

An interesting study was made by Alliant in running a *Computer Aided Engineering*
(CAE) program ANSYS, performing finite element analysis. The program was run on
different FX/8 (see Chapter 7) configurations consisting of a single processor (one CE),
two CEs, three CEs and so on up to the maximal eight CEs. The number of jobs per
hour was noted on the vertical axis, while the corresponding system cost is noted on
the horizontal, resulting in the graph shown in Figure 13.1. The figure clearly shows
the performance; cost (in thousands of dollars) points for each of the eight possible
configurations. These results are compared in the same graph with those of other systems:
Convex, IBM 4381 and VAX 8800 (a dual processor). While the performance of a
single CE is about 50% of the Convex and comparable to the IBM 4381, its cost is
about 25% of the IBM 4381 and 50% of the Convex. The two CE Alliant has a performance
no lower than the others, at a considerably lower cost. Only the Convex-XP model has
a performance comparable to two CEs, at almost double cost.

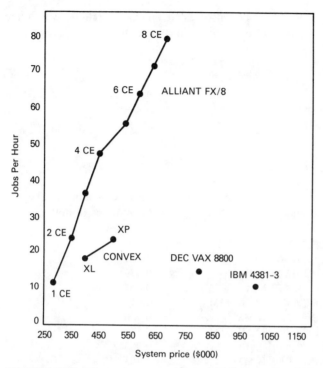

FIGURE 13.1. Throughput–mechanical CAE (courtesy of Alliant Computer Sys. Corp.).

A benchmark comparison of the Alliant, ELXSI, Convex and some VAX models, using a suite of 33 DR Labs. benchmarks, was reported in [1]. The geometric mean time (sec.) for all benchmarks was:

VAX 8650	1.584
Alliant, 1 CE	1.480
VAX 8700	1.469
ELXSI 6420	1.193
Convex (vector mode) XP	0.487

For the above benchmarks the ELXSI 6420 CPU performed better than the Alliant CE and the VAX models tested. The Alliant CE performance came out between the VAX models, at a value close to that of the VAX 8700. The comparative performance with respect to the Convex fits the results in Figure 13.1, obtained with a different benchmark. The above results were also normalized with respect to the performance of a Micro VAX II (assumed to be 1.0):

Micro VAX II	1.00
VAX 8650	5.79
Alliant, 1 CE	6.19
VAX 8700	6.24
ELXSI 6420	7.68
Convex (vector mode) XP	19.10

The previous benchmarks were also tested on configurations with more processors. The total computing time (sec.) for all benchmarks was:

ELXSI 6420, 3 CPUs	25
Alliant, 8 CEs	45
Alliant, 4 CEs	55
Convex (vector mode) XP	64
ELXSI 6420, 1 CPU	66
VAX 8700	74
VAX 8650	78
Alliant, 1 CE	109

ELXSI comes out with a definite edge in the above comparison. The cost of some of the above configurations (as reported in [1]) is (in millions of dollars)

Alliant FX/1, 1 CE, 2 IPs, 16MB MM	0.099
Convex XP, 1 CPU, 16 MB MM	0.475
ELXSI 6420, 1 CPU, 16 MB MM	0.479
VAX 8700, 1 CPU, 32 MB MM	0.601
Alliant FX/8, 4 CEs, 6 IPs, 32 MB MM	0.617
ELXSI 6422, 2 CPUs, 32 MB MM	0.730
Alliant FX/8, 8 CEs, 6 IPs, 32 MB MM	0.813
VAX 8800, 2 CPUs (8700), 48 MB MM	0.905
ELXSI 6424, 4 CPUs, 64 MB MM	1.163
Alliant FX/8, 8 CEs, 12 IPs, 256 MB MM	1.951
VAX 8974, 4 CPUs (8700), 128 MB MM	2.810

where MM = Main Memory, MB = Mega Bytes.

Combining performance with cost, we have the basis to compare a single ELXSI 6420 CPU with a single Alliant CE, both having the same main memory size. The first combined figure will be:

(Total benchmarks time) * (Cost)—
     Alliant, 1 CE $109 * 0.099 = 10.8$
     ELXSI, 1 CPU (6420) $66 * 0.479 = 31.6$

The second combined figure:

(Performance relative to Micro VAX II)/(Cost)—
     Alliant, 1 CE $6.19/0.099 = 62$
     ELXSI, 1 CPU (6420) $7.68/0.470 = 16$

While the ELXSI processor (6420) has a definite raw performance edge over the Alliant CE, the combined cost-performance figure favors the Alliant by a factor of over three to one. The ELXSI 6420 performance runs from 25% to 65% above that of the CE. It should be noted tha the above results are based on a finite number of selected benchmarks. They are indicative but certainly not conclusive. Similar results, comparing a three CPU (6420) ELXSI system with VAX 8700, were also reported in [2].

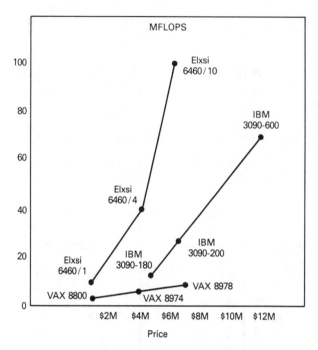

FIGURE 13.2. ELXSI 6460 performance/price comparison (courtesy of ELXSI Corp.).

Cost-performance comparisons, using the Linpack 64-bit benchmark, between the ELXSI 6460 (Pegasus) and other systems have also been reported [3]. The results of the comparison are shown in Figure 13.2. The performance (in MFLOPS) for configurations of a single, four and 10 CPUs (6460) are plotted along the vertical axis, with the cost (in millions of $) reflected along the horizontal. The comparison is made with models of the IBM 3090 and the VAX. The 3090–200 has two CPUs and the 3090-600 has six. The VAX 8800 has two CPUs (8700), the 8974 has four, and the 8978 has eight. The ELXSI 6460/10 performance is superior to all systems compared, while maintaining a lower cost than VAX 8978, IBM 3090-200 and certainly IBM 3090-600. A cost-performance comparison, using the Linpack benchmark [7,8], between ELXSI 6420 configurations and other systems (Alliant, VAX, IBM 3090, Multiflow, SCS-40, Convex), is shown in Figure 13.3. As expected, the eight CPU configuration of ELXSI 6420 exceeds that of Alliant FX/8 (eight CEs) by almost an order of magnitude, however the cost of the Alliant is considerably lower (note that Figure 13.3 has a logarithmic scale on both axes). A similar diagram, using the same Linpack benchmark, shown in Figure 13.4, is offered by IPM, the manufacturer of IP-1. According to this benchmark test, the IP-1 outperforms all other systems, shown in the graph, while being at the almost lowest cost (except for two systems). Of course, experimentation based on a single benchmark is by far inconclusive.

Similar studies, using the Whetstone and Dhrystone benchmarks, investigating the increase in performance as a function of the number of configured processors, have been conducted by Sequent Computer Systems, Inc., for its Symmetry system (see

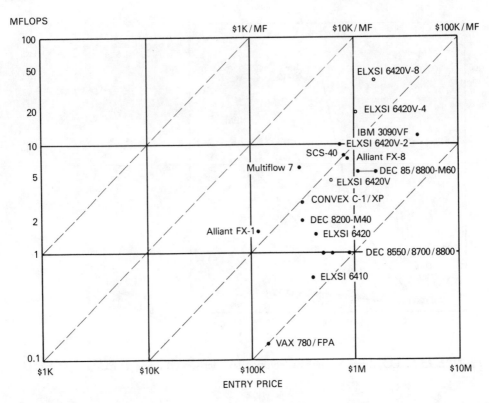

FIGURE 13.3. Linpack 64-bit benchmark price-performance comparisons (courtesy of ELXSI Corp.).

section 8.2) [4]. The Whetstone benchmark is an industry standard test for measuring the floating point performance of computer systems. Speed is expressed in *Millions of Whetstone Instructions per second* (MWhets). Figure 13.5 shows the cumulative MWhets achieved by Symmetry systems with varying numbers of processors (along the horizontal axis). Results for both single (32 bit) and double precision (64 bits) variations of the program are shown. The single precision results are compared to the performance of the VAX 8800 dual processor, running under the VMS OS. The dual precision performance is compared to that of VAX 8800, IBM 3090-200 (two CPUs) and the Cray X-MP (four CPUs). In single precision, four Symmetry CPUs are needed to equal the performance of the VAX 8800. In double precision the number of Symmetry CPUs needed to obtain equal performance is:

VAX 8800	3
IBM 3090–200	11
Cray X-MP	15

It should be kept in mind that while the Sequent Symmetry, whose CPUs are Intel 80386 microprocessors, is actually a multimicroprocessor, the VAX 8800 is in the

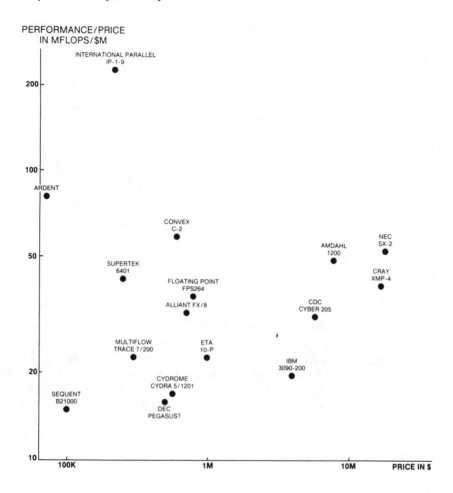

PERFORMANCE/PRICE
IN MFLOPS/$M

FIGURE 13.4. Linpack price performance comparisons on a log/log scale (courtesy of IPM, Inc.)

supermini category, while the IBM 3090 and Cray X-MP are considered to be *supercomputers*.

An interesting detail about the Whetstone benchmark program is that it consists of 211 lines of FORTRAN and compiles into an executable file of about 37 KBytes. Thus, the entire program and its data fit into the 64 KByte cache of each Symmetry processor, assuring a 100% hit ratio during the execution of the benchmark. The benchmark experiment was run in a ''multistream'' fashion, by loading a copy of the benchmark program into each processor cache, participating in the experiment. The cumulative

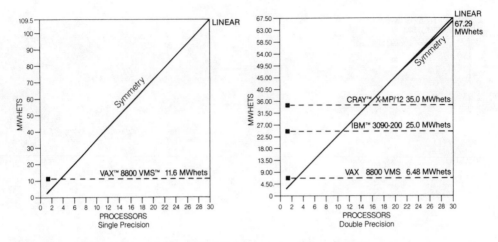

FIGURE 13.5. Symmetry Whetstone performance (courtesy of Sequent Computer Sys. Corp.)

Whetstone performance is the sum of the MWhets achieved by the multiple programs.

The Dhrystone benchmark [9] is an industry standard test for measuring the integer performance of computer systems. Speed is expressed in *Dhrystones per Second*. The Dhrystone benchmark consists of 309 lines of C and compiles into an executable file of about 44 KBytes, fitting into a Symmetry processor cache. The Dhrystone benchmark was run in a "multistream" fashion, similarly to the Whetstones. The results are shown in Figure 13.6. The performance is compared to that of VAX 8650, IBM 3090-200 and Amdahl 5890/300E. The number of Symmetry processors needed to attain equal performance to the above systems is:

FIGURE 13.6. Symmetry Dhrystone performance (courtesy of Sequent Computer Sys. Corp.).

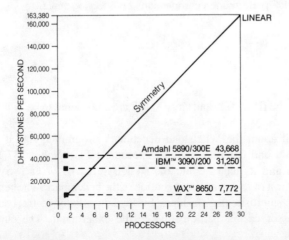

VAX 8650	2
IBM 3090–200	6
Amdahl 5890/300E	8

Quite an impressive performance of a multimicroprocessor compared to mainframe super-computers.

A different set of benchmarks was used by FPS to compare its T-Series (see section 9.3) n-cube system with the Cray X-MP[5, 6]. The results featuring the T/100 (64 nodes) and the T/200 (128 nodes), expressed in MFLOPS, are shown in Table 13.4. The relative results differ considerably for different benchmark programs.

TABLE 13.4. Benchmark performance comparison between FPS T-series and the Cray X-MP.

Benchmark	T/100	T/200	Performance in MFLOPS Cray X-MP-48
Matrix Multiply	596	1125	600
2 D Convolution	579	1157	810
2 D Wave	232	462	500
Linear Solver	81	130	796
2 D FFT	47	60	370

A performance comparison analysis between crossbar, multistage interconnection and multibus networks (see Chapter 2), was recently reported [10]. As should have been expected, the crossbar network has a clear edge as far as the probability of a memory request being accepted and the memory bandwidth are concerned. It would take an eight-bus multibus system to top the multistage network. Comparing the processor utilization, the crossbar and the multistage network are very close, with the crossbar having a slight edge. Multibus systems with up to four buses rate lower. All of the above comparative analysis was performed on synchronous systems.

References

1. J. A. Steinberg, "A New Twist: Vectors in Parallel," *Digital Review*, June 29, 1987, pp. 63–66.

2. J. A. Steinberg, "A Virtual VAX Does It In Parallel," *Digital Review*, March 23, 1987.

3. W. Brandel, "Elxsi's Pegasus Will Fly Above All The Rest at 250 VAX MIPS," *Digital Review*, Feb. 8, 1988.

4. Sequent Computer Systems Inc., *Tech. Notes—Symmetry*, 1988.

5. D. Miles et al., "Specification and Performance Analysis of Six Benchmark Programs for the FPS T-series," FPS Inc. *Report*, 1986.

6. J. Gustafson, S. Hawkinson, "A Language-independent Set of Benchmarks for Parallel Processors," *FPS Inc. Report*, March 1986.

7. J. J. Dongarra, J. R. Bunch, C. B. Boler, G. W. Stewart, *LINPACK Users' Guide*, SIAM Publications, Philadelphia, PA, 1979.

8. J. J. Dongarra, "Performance of Various Computers Using Standard Linear Equations Software in a FORTRAN Environment," *Computer Architecture News*, Vol. 13, No. 1, pp. 3–9, March 1985.

9. R. P. Weicker, "Dhrystone, a Synthetic Systems Programming Benchmark," *Comm. ACM*, Vol. 27, No. 10, Oct. 1984.

10. L. N. Bhuyan, Q. Yang, D. P. Agrawal, "Performance of Multiprocessor Interconnection Networks," *IEEE Computer*, Vol. 22, No. 2, pp. 25–37, Feb. 1989.

CHAPTER 14

Real-time Multiprocessing

14.1   The Concept of Real-time

Real-time computing systems can be defined as computing systems required to yield results at specific deadlines during actual implementation [1, 2]. Real-time systems can be *interactive* meaning that where an operator at a terminal expects an immediate response before taking the next step in the operation. Real-time systems are utilized in many cases as *process control systems*, where a computer is directing or monitoring an ongoing physical process.

Real-time systems are applied in a variety of areas. Industrial real-time applications may involve control of chemical processes, machine control, data acquisition for medical equipment, for power systems, and for avionics. Real-time military applications may include field command-control-communications (C-cube) systems, instrument panels and monitoring systems. Real-time computing systems are also used in the managment and handling of satellite communications. In the office-business market real-time systems are used for airline reservation operations, data acquisition for financial transactions, control of laser copiers and printers and many other applications.

No matter what is the nature of the application, *timing* (or rather obtaining the results on time) is one of the most crucial issues in real-time systems. The real-time computing system receives, periodically, a certain amount of input signals in the form of operator requests from a terminal or from sensor measurements. The input signals undergo processing by the computing system, according to algorithms, appropriate for the application, yielding a set of output results. The output results may appear as messages on a terminal screen or as signals directed to various locations of the system. These output signals must be made available by a prescribed deadline. Any tardiness would result in a faulty operation of the system. The output results should be held available for a sufficient time for the rest of the system to act upon them. Once the results have been used and acted upon, space for new results of the next cycle should be provided.

Based on the above considerations we can define the following *timing measures*, that can be applied to real-time systems:

- *Response time*—time the real-time system takes to recognize and respond to an external event. To be more precise, the time interval between the appearance of an input signal and the appearance of an output result.

- *Survival time*—time during which output data will remain available to be noticed and acted upon.

- *Throughput*—total number of events which the system can handle in a given time period. When measured in bits/sec., it is called *bandwidth*.

- *Recovery time* (*cleanup time*)—that time it takes to provide space for the output results of the next cycle after having acquired and acted upon the previous results.

Of the above timing measures, the response time is the most crucial for real-time applications. Its value, compared to the required information update period, will establish whether a given computing system is fit for a specific real-time implementation.

Let us now look more closely at the specific tasks that a real-time computing system would usually be required to perform. It should also be noted that the organization, implementing the real-time system, may have additional computational tasks, not necessarily connected with the real-time operation. We can, therefore, classify the tasks in the following manner.

1. Direct real-time tasks repeated at specified time periods (sometimes called sampling periods):

   (a) Acquisition of input variables through sensors, keyboard or other devices. In many cases, the input signals must undergo an additional transformation, in order to be treatable by the computing system (such as A/D conversion, sampling and hold).

   (b) Application of computational algorithms by the processing subsystem. The algorithms depend on the nature of the real-time operation. The worst case computing time of the algorithms should be below the operational sampling period.

   (c) Transmission of output results to the terminals and/or control points. This may require in many cases transformation operations such as processing for video display and D/A conversion.

2. Indirect tasks associated with the real-time operation, such as diagnostics, memory check, non real-time update of process status. The results of these tasks are not expected at specific deadlines, however they are still to be performed to assure reliable operation and maintenance of the system.

3. Non real-time tasks or computational tasks required by the organization, implementing the real-time system, but unrelated to the real-time operation.

As we can see, the computing system, managing the real-time operation, is called to perform a great variety of tasks, some of which are to be performed periodically (tasks 1(a), (b), and (c)), within prescribed periods of time. If the computing system is dedicated exclusively to the real-time operation (that is no tasks in category 3), if the indirect tasks are kept to a minimum (a very small number of category 2 tasks) and if the sampling periods are relatively long, one can fulfill all tasks with a relatively low cost computing system (such as the VAX 11/750 or other comparable systems). The more tasks are required of the system and the shorter the sampling period, the more powerful, faster, and more expensive will the computing system have to be. Eventually, with the increase of the requirements, the cost of the required computing system may reach a point, sufficient to render the real-time implementation uneconomical and, therefore, unimplementable in practice.

The above consideration brings us to the following: instead of using a powerful and expensive single-processor computer, why not assign the numerous tasks to a number of relatively simpler and inexpensive processors? Each processor will be required to perform only a part of the necessary tasks. Thus, the timing constraints imposed on each processor will be less stringent, permitting the use of less powerful, lower cost processors. Since all of the above processors will be engaged in the overall management of a specific system, they cannot be separate computers. They must necessarily be coordinated, synchronized, interconnected and endowed with a capability of shared storage of information (shared memory). In other words, they should be configured into a *multipro-cessor* [3–5].

The recent appearance of relatively low cost, fast and efficient, easily programmable, commercial multiprocessors (see Part Two), makes the implementation of high-throughput, short response time, multiple-task real-time systems, an economically feasible reality [6–8].

14.2   *Application of Multiprocessors in Real-time Systems*

Let us now apply a multiprocessor to a real-time system. Let us first assume that the multiprocessor is dedicated to the management of the real-time system only and there are no other tasks (no type 3 tasks). To be specific, let us take a four-processor system. Taking into account that modern commercial multiprocessors have from eight to over 100 processors (see Part Two), this would be a modest and relatively inexpensive configuration. The task assignment between the processors, designated as P1, P2, P3, P4, can be as follows:

P1:   Acquisition and initial processing of input variables (1(a)).
P2:   Running the computational algorithms (1(b)).
P3:   Processing and transmission of output variables (1(c)).
P4:   Running of the indirect tasks (2).

A block diagram of the system is shown in Figure 14.1.

It should be noted that the operation of the different processors is not disjoint. There is a constant need of communication of information between them, contributing to an overall system overhead in the multiprocessor [5]. This creates a special problem in multiprocessor implementation; it was discussed at the end of Chapter 2.

As the number of variables grows, the algorithms become more complicated and time consuming, and as the sampling period decreases, even four processors may not be sufficient to do the job, within certain economic constraints (which always exist). In the modern commercial multiprocessors (many of which are really multimicroproces-sors), expanding the system to add more processors is relatively simple and the cost is reasonable (see Chapter 13). Additional tasks, unrelated to the real-time application (3), can also be accomodated. We can, therefore, generalize the above processor assign-ment:

P1, P2, . . . ,PA: Tasks of type Ia, in parallel.
PA+1, . . . ,PB: Tasks of type Ib.
PB+1, . . . ,PC: Tasks of type Ic.
PC+1, . . . ,PD: Tasks of type II.
PD+1, . . . ,PN: Tasks of type III.

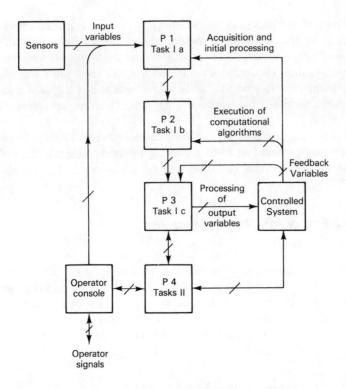

FIGURE 14.1. A four-processor real-time system.

where N is the maximal number of processors in a multiprocessor configuration. In particular, tasks of a certain type may be still accomodated by a single processor, and some processors may handle tasks of more than one type. The above schedule is only an example out of many different possibilities.

The configuration, illustrated in Figure 14.1, could be successfully realized using either an Alliant FX/4 or FX/40 (four CEs, four ACEs), described in Chapter 7, or a four CPU ELXSI configuration of 6420s or 6460s. Based on the data in Chapter 13, if speed/performance is most important, and cost is not a major consideration, the priority of selection should be (the first listed has the highest priority):

1. ELXSI 6464;

2. ELXSI 6424;

3. Alliant FX/40; and

4. Alliant FX/4.

If on the other hand, the cost is of primary consideration, the above ordering should be reversed. Another important qualification is that the above ordering reflects integer computation performance. If *floating point performance* is the primary consideration, the ordering should be:

1. Alliant FX/40;

2. Alliant FX/4;

3. ELXSI 6464;

4. ELXSI 6424.

Both Alliant (see Chapter 7) and ELXSI (see section 8.1) offer efficient OS support for real-time operations.

Naturally, other systems, described in Part Two, could also be used in real-time applications. The above comparison between Alliant and ELXSI was chosen as an example. The same considerations could be repeated for the other systems as well.

14.3 Real-time OS

The special requirements of multiprocessor OS have been discussed in Chapter 4. These requirements should also hold for multiprocessors implemented in real-time applications. There are however additional requirements for satisfactory real-time operation. In real-time systems, the OS and the application are more tightly interwined than in other systems [9]. One of the most important problems is how to provide high level abstractions for real-time programmers, and yet meet *timing* considerations which are fundamentally dependent on the implementation and environment. In addition, almost all resource management techniques, used in existing OS, are not designed to guarantee that a program's critical timing constraints can be met. Some important real-time OS issues include:

(a) *Time-driven resource management.* Traditionally, when many tasks are waiting for access to a shared resource, the allocation policy is to provide access in FIFO (First In, First Out) order. However, this policy totally ignores the tasks' timing constraints. Time-driven allocation policies must be developed that can meet the real-time scheduling requirements. Such management policies should be applied not only for the processor, but also for memory, I/O and communication resources.

(b) *Problem-specific OS facilities.* A real-time OS' functions should be able to adapt to a variety of user and system needs. For instance, a real-time OS should provide a separation between scheduling policy and mechanism. Thus, a user can choose or the system can select the time-driven resource management algorithm most suitable for a particular application or situation.

(c) *Integrated system-wide scheduling support.* Real-time scheduling principles must be applied to system resources, application tasks, and OS' overall design. In particular, a focussed effort is necessary to integrate real-time communication with real-time processor scheduling, and with real-time database support for a large, complex real-time computer system. For a sequence of actions to meet a *deadline*, precedence constraints must be satisfied and resources must be available *in time* for each action of the sequence. Inopportune delays at any stage of the process can cause missed deadlines.

(d) *Predictability*. The OS should provide the real time system with a predictability capability, that is, the system's functional and timing behavior should be as deterministic as is necessary to satisfy system specifications.

As far as distributed real-time systems are concerned [10], the key problem in system management is the lack of integrated system-wide approaches to managing task, message and database *transaction latencies*. It is not sufficient to provide latency management in processors and ignore it in the network that is the integrating element of the system. This is especially true for those systems with processing threads that span multiple processors and hard end-to-end response requirements. The shared resources which must be scheduled using time-driven techniques (such as rate-monotonic scheduling) include as a minimum: CPUs, database coprocessors, network interface units, I/O channels, buses, and disks.

References 1. S. Savitzky, *Real-time Microprocessor Systems*, Van Nostrand Reingold, NY, 1985.

2. E. H. Dummermuth, "Distributed Real-time Control," *Proc. IFAC Distributed Control Systems Symp.*, pp. 63–67, 1985.

3. K. Hwang, F. A. Briggs, *Parallel Processing and Computer Architecture*, McGraw-Hill, NY, 1984.

4. J. P. Hayes, *Computer Architecture and Organization*, 2nd ed., McGraw-Hill, NY, 1988.

5. H. S. Stone, *High-Performance Computer Architecture*, Addison-Wesley, Reading, MA, 1987.

6. J. Bond, "Parallel-processing Concepts Finally Come Together in Real Systems," *Computer Design*, June 1, 1987, pp. 51–74.

7. N. Mokhoff, "Parallelism Breeds a New Class of Supercomputers," *Computer Design*, March 15, 1987, pp. 53–64.

8. D. Tabak, "Real-time Multiprocessors," in J. Zalewski, W. Ehrenberger, eds., *Hardware and Software for Real-time Process Control*, pp. 363–372, North-Holland, Amsterdam, 1989.

9. J. A. Stankovic, "Misconceptions About Real-time Computing," *IEEE Computer*, Vol. 21, No. 10, pp. 10–19, Oct. 1988.

10. P. H. Watson, "An Overview of Architectural Directions for Real-time Distributed Systems," *Proc. 5th Workshop on RTSOS*, pp. 59–65, Washington, D.C., May 1988.

CHAPTER 15

Concluding Comments

After discussing the principles of multiprocessor architecture, structure, design, software and operating systems in Part One, a selected set of modern commercial multiprocessors was presented in Part Two. The design features implemented in existing multiprocessors were summarized in Part Three, along with some comparative data. Real-time application of multiprocessors was also discussed.

As argued in Chapter 1, the multiprocessor (the MIMD-type system) is only a particular case of a parallel processing computing system. Other types of such systems have been under constant development in the academia and industry yielding powerful commercial products.

One of the widely implemented parallel processing techniques is arithmetic pipeline vector processing. Arithmetic pipelines are particularly efficient in handling large-scale vector operands. One of the latest examples in this category is the *Floating Point Systems* (FPS) M64/145 Application Accelerator. It is a 64-bit parallel pipeline system, extendable to 15 accelerator modules for a total peak performance of 341 MFLOPS. It is compatible for interface configuration with DEC, IBM, Unisys and Apollo systems.

Another notable example of widespread parallel processing systems are the SIMD *Array Processors* (see Chapter 1). Notable examples are the *Thinking Machine* and the *Massively Parallel Processor* (MPP) with thousands of elementary parallel elements (PEs) working in unison. The large-scale SIMD systems have achieved a considerable success in solving problems in astronomy, chemistry, metereology, image processing, and other areas.

The individual processors of SIMD systems and their control unit are relatively simple. On the other hand, the design of MIMDs is much more complicated (see Chapter 5) and results in a highly complex and relatively costly (per processor) system. The question inevitably arises: what should be the primary direction of future development of massive parallelism, SIMD, or MIMD?

While SIMD systems are easier to realize in massive (thousands) quantities of processors, they have a high-utilization factor for only a limited class of problems. There are many problems, a large part of which is sequential in nature. They cannot be decomposed for an efficient solution on an SIMD. On the other hand, an MIMD can handle a number of programs, executed on its processors, which can perform different operations simultaneously (unlike the SIMD PEs). Even if we have a non-decomposable sequential problem, it can be scheduled to run on one CPU, while the other CPUs can be allocated to other programs, as it is done on the Alliant, for instance (see Chapter 7).

Despite of the higher cost and complexity, the development of larger-scale MIMD systems will continue because of their generality and universality. As the final chapters of this text are being written, Ametek has announced a new 1024-node (processor) Series 2010 multiprocessor. Each node is based on an MC68020 microprocessor (see section 11.2), whose performance is 4MIPS and 0.63 MFLOPS, with an MC68882 Floating Point Unit. Each node can have an optional Vector Floating Point Accelerator (VFPA) for a 10 MIPS and 20 MFLOPS performance per node. The Linpack benchmark performance is seven MFLOPS per VFPA node (see Chapter 13). The overall peak performance of a fully configured 2010 (1024 nodes) is 20 GFLOPS. The nodes are interconnected by a two-dimensional, message-passing Giga Link network. New MIMD systems are under constant development.

We may see in the future, hybrid combinations of massive SIMD—MIMD systems. Clusters of array processors (SIMD) can be interconnected to form a combined MIMD system, under central control. Each SIMD cluster will be able to execute a different program. Separate clusters could be modularly combined into a single SIMD, if necessary. The new systems should certainly be flexibly reconfigurable. The SIMD clusters could also be alternately configured as a distributed network. The development of efficient systems of the above category definitely constitutes an interesting and important problem for future research.

Although a large number of commercial multiprocessors has been manufactured, the overall problem of multiprocessor design is far from being completely solved. More research should be done in perfecting many aspects of multiprocessor construction and utilization, particularly in the areas of software and algorithm development. Some possible paths for future additional research involving multiprocessors are:

(a) Development of methods of automatic partitioning of HLL programs at a refined level of granularity.

(b) Development of concurrent HLL compilers.

(c) Further development of multiprocessor OS.

(d) Development of efficient interconnection networks, reducing bottlenecks and memory latency.

(e) Improving cache coherence mechanisms.

(f) Developing efficient parallel processing algorithms for different applications areas.

Successful ventures in the above research areas will eventually yield even more powerful, fast and efficient parallel processors, possibly combining MIMD, SIMD and certainly vector processing features (vector processing features are already offered in a number of multiprocessor CPUs). The basic speed of processing, from the technology point of view, is limited by the speed of light. However, the increase in overall throughput by exploiting parallelism is limited only by our current abilities, perceptions and imagination. Expanding those limits by continuing multiprocessor research and development will undoubtedly bring its rewards by endowing humanity with computing capabilities which, for the moment, are in the realm of science fiction but will become the reality of tomorrow.

Abbreviations List

ACE	Advanced Computational Element
ACT	Access Control Table
ACTE	Access Control Table Entry
ALU	Arithmetic Logic Unit
ATU	Address Translation Unit
BSP	Burroughs Scientific Processor
CAE	Computer Aided Engineering
CAS	Compare and Swap
CCU	Concurrency Control Unit
CDC	Control Data Corporation
CE	Computational Element
CMMU	Cache Memory Management Unit
COVI	Concurrent Outer Vector Inner
CPU	Control Processing Unit
CSU	Common Storage Area
CU	Control Unit
DARPA	Defense Advanced Research Projects Agency
DEC	Digital Equipment Corporation
DRAM	Dynamic RAM
FAA	Fetch And Add
FPCR	Floating Point Control Register
FPSR	Floating Point Status Register
GFLOPS	Giga Floating Point Operations Per Second (1000 MFLOPS)
HLL	High-level Language
HPO	High-performance Option
IBM	International Business Machines
I/O	Input/Output
IOP	Input–Output Processor
IP	Interactive Processor
IPC	Interprocessor Communication
ISO	International Standards Organization
JCL	Job Control Language
LAN	Local Area Network
LM	Local Memory
LNS	Local Name Space
M	Memory
MAM	Multi Access Memory
MFLOPS	Millions of Floating Point Operations Per Second
MIMD	Multiple Instructions Multiple Data

MIPS	Millions of Instructions Per Second
MISD	Multiple Instructions Single Data
MM	Main Memory
MOL	Message-oriented Languages
MPP	Massively Parallel Processor
NFS	Network File System
NYU	New York University
OOL	Operation-oriented Languages
PCB	Process Control Block
PFN	Page Frame Number
POL	Procedure-oriented Languages
PSD	Process State Descriptor
PT	Page Table
PTE	Page Table Entry
RAM	Random Access Memory
RMW	Read Modify Write
RO	Read Only
ROM	Read Only Memory
R/W, RW	Read–Write
RWM	Read–Write Memory
SCCS	Source Code Control System
SDA	Supervisor Data ACTE
SIMD	Single Instruction Multiple Data
SISD	Single Instruction Single Data
SPA	Supervisor Program ACTE
ST	Segment Table
STE	Segment Table Entry
TAS	Test And Set
TB	Translation Buffer
TCP	Transmission Control Protocol
TLB	Translation Lockaside Buffer
TSS	Task State Segment
TSSR	Task State Segment Register
UCC	Ultra Cache Card
UDA	User Data ACTE
UDP	User Diagram Protocol
UIC	Ultra Interface Card
UPA	User Program ACTE
W/R	Write/Read

Glossary

addressing mode. The way in which an operand is specified, or the way in which the effective address of an instruction operand is calculated.

arithmetic logic unit (ALU). The component of a computer where arithmetic and logic operations are performed.

array. A set or list of elements, usually variables of data.

array system. An array is generally understood to be a collection of N processors, P_1, . . . ,P_n, handling the same instruction issued by a single control unit. Each processor, P_i, is equipped with a local memory, M_i, used by P_i for storing both its operands and the computational results it obtains. An array composed of N processors may concurrently execute N identical operations with one program instruction. Each instruction handles a data vector made of operands handled by P_1, . . . P_n, respectively. An array of N processors thus implements data parallellism but no instruction parallelism.

assembler. A program which translates symbolic opcodes into machine language and assigns memory locations for variables and constants.

assembly language. The machine-oriented programming language used by an assembly system.

bandwidth. The number of bits per second that can be handled or transferred by a resource (such as a bus).

barrier. A synchronization point; all processes wait at the barrier until the last process arrives, at which time all processes proceed.

base address. A given address from which an absolute address is derived by combination with a relative address.

cache. A relatively small capacity (compared to main memory), high-speed buffer memory.

cache coherence. The state that exists when all caches within a multiprocessor have identical values for any shared variable that is simultaneously in two or more caches.

catastrophic failure. A failure within a system causing a complete breakdown and a cessation of its operation.

coarse-grain parallelism. Parallel execution in which the amount of computation per task is several times larger than the overhead and communication expended per task.

compiler. A code that translates a program written in a High-level Language (HLL) into an object program.

context switch. The process of saving the state of one task and restoring the state of a second task to enable a computer system to change execution from one task to another.

control-driven. Architecture with one or more program counters that determine the order in which instructions are executed.

control unit (CU). The unit responsible for sequencing, fetching, decoding and producing all of the necessary control signals to execute an instruction in a computer.

CPU (Central processing unit). The unit of a computing system that includes the circuits controlling the interpretation and execution of instructions and the ALU.

critical section. A section of a program that can be executed by at most one process at a time.

crossbar. An interconnection in which each input is connected to each output through a path that contains a single switching node.

crosspoint. A switching node in a crossbar that connects a single input to a single output.

data-driven. Data flow architecture in which execution of instructions depends on availability of operands.

data flow. An architecture in which the sequence of instruction execution depends not on a program counter, but on the availability of data.

deadlock. The state in which two or more processes are deferred indefinitely because each process is awaiting another process to make progress, and no process releases any resources it holds.

decoder (n-to2^n). A multiple output combinational logic network with n input lines and 2^n output lines. For each possible input condition one and only one signal will be logic 1.

delayed branch. A branch instruction that defers altering the flow of control until one more instruction that follows it has completed execution.

demand-driven. Data flow architecture in which execution of an instruction depends upon both availability of its operands and a request for the result.

dependent loop. A loop in which the operations in each iteration depend on the results of previous iterations.

destination address. Address of a storage location in Memory or a register, into which an information item is to be stored.

direct addressing. An addressing mode using an absolute address within the instruction.

dynamic scheduling. A method that allows processes to be scheduled during run time.

effective addressing. The address obtained after indirect or indexing modifications are calculated.

fine-grain parallelism. A form of parallel execution in which the amount of work per task is small compared to the amount of work per task required for communication and other overhead.

granularity. A measure of the size of an individual task to be executed on a parallel processor.

high-level languages (HLL). Problem oriented languages such as Pascal, PL/1, Ada, FORTRAN, Algol, Cobol, which have a powerful set of operational and control statements which are substantially above the basic statement types provided in assembly languages. In conventional computers, transformed into assembly languages by a compiler.

hot-spot contention. An interference phenomenon observed in multiprocessors due to simultaneous, competitive memory accesses by a number of processes.

hypercube. A parallel processor whose interconnection structure treats individual processors as the nodes of a multidimensional cube and interconnects two processors if the corresponding nodes of the cube are adjacent.

immediate addressing. An addressing mode where the operand is actually a part of the instruction.

index register. A register used to contain an address offset.

indexed addressing. An addressing mode where the effective address is calculated by adding the contents of a special register, called an ''index register'' to another address value, given in the direct or any other mode.

indirect address. An address in a computer instruction which indicates a location where the address of the referenced operand is to be found.

instruction execution. The process of actually executing the instruction by the CPU, after it has been decoded.

instruction fetch. The process of the transfer (move) of the instruction from its Memory storage into the CPU, and its decoding (some texts put the decoding within the instruction execution period).

interleaved memory. Memory divided into a number of modules or banks that can be accessed simultaneously.

interlock. A control device or signal that defers the execution of one function until a conflicting function has completed execution.

interrupt. An event that changes the normal flow of instruction execution. Generally external to the process executing when the interrupt occurs.

I/O port. A junction between the main bus and the I/O device. It is a part of a device interface; a group of bits accessed by the processor during I/O operations.

latch. A logic circuit to which an input action must be applied to a specified input to cause the device to assume one of two logic conditions. Further application of the latch input signal has no effect; the latch remains in the latched position. Release of the latch must be accomplished by application of an input signal to another input location.

latency. The delay between the request for information and the time the information is supplied to the requester.

local memory. The private memory directly connected to a processor in a parallel computer.

lock. A semaphore which ensures that only one process at a time can access a shared data structure or execute a critical section of code.

machine language. Information that can be directly processed by the computer.

master controller. In a multiprocessing system, one of the subsystems which assumes control of all the others.

memory-to-memory organization of the processor. An organization in which each instruction has its operands fetched from the memory and the result is sent back to the memory.

microoperation. The most elementary processing done in a computer consists of executing a microoperation during a word transfer between registers. To execute a microoperation, a data path between registers must contain the control circuit and may or may not contain an execution circuit. An execution circuit implements a Boolean function that transforms input data word(s) stored in one or several source registers into an output data word broadcast to one or several destination registers. Since a microoperation necessarily includes one control circuit, it is activated by the microcommand that opens this control circuit.

multiple instruction multiple data (MIMD). A parallel processing configuration where multiple processors execute different processes simultaneously.

multiprocessing. Utilization of several computers or processors to logically or functionally divide jobs or programs, and to execute them simultaneously.

multiprogramming. Execution of two or more programs in core at the same time. Execution cycles between programs.

multitasking. A programming technique that allows a single application to consist of multiple tasks, executing concurrently.

opcode. The pattern of bits within an instruction that specify the operation to be performed.

operand. A quantity which is affected, manipulated or operated upon.

overflow. The state in which a numerical value exceeds the maximum representable numerical value.

overhead. Time and computation not spent in calculating the result of a program. Examples: data initialization, I/O, synchronization, communication.

parallel processing. Simultaneous execution, or any other treatment, of more than one instruction, or more than one data item at a time.

Parallel system. A parallel system generally means a system that implements either instruction parallelism, or both types of parallelism, instruction and data, in a single system.

Partitioning. The process of grouping related portions of programs together to force them to reside in contiguous regions of memory so that they tend to be transferred together among the levels of a memory hierarchy.

Perfect-shuffle interconnection. An interconnection structure that connects processors according to a permutation that corresponds to a perfect shuffle of a deck of cards.

Physical memory. Actual memory configured in hardware. Synonymous with Real Memory.

Pipeline system. A pipeline system is a parallel system containing N pipelines. Since each pipeline computes one instruction sequence in the overlapped mode, a pipeline system may compute N instruction sequences concurrently and thus implement instruction parallelism. No data parallelism is implemented since each instruction handles no more than two operands at a time.

pipelining. In general pipelining requires partitioning of the instruction into several phases and allows for the overlapped execution of consecutive phases assigned to consecutive instructions. If the instruction is partitioned into k phases, F_1, F_2, . . . ,F_k, then the pipeline that executes it contains k stages, S_1, S_2, . . . ,S_k, so that S_i executes phase F_i, of the instruction, etc.

procedure. The course of action taken for the solution of a problem.

process. The smallest unit of programming activity which can be scheduled to run on a processor.

processing element (PE). A general purpose ALU capable of executing a conventional instruction set.

processor. A physical device performing data processing tasks.

program. The counter sequence of instructions and routines necessary to solve a problem.

program counter (PC). The counter that stores a current (macro-) instruction address in the main memory.

register transfer notation (language). A method which describes the information flow and processing tasks among the data stored in registers of a computer system. Uses a set of expressions and statements which resemble the statements used in programming languages.

relative address. The number that specifies the difference between the actual address and a base address.

reliability, R(t). The probability that a given systems will continue to function faultlessly up to a time t.

scalable architecture. An architecture is scalable if increasing the number of processors, or other resources, produces an analogous increase in the processing power of the machine.

semaphore. Shared data structure used to synchronize the actions of multiple cooperating processes.

single instruction multiple data (SIMD). A parallel processing configuration where multiple Processing Elements (PE) perform the same instruction on different data simultaneously.

single-address instruction. An instruction whose format contains a single operand address reference.

software. The collection of programs and routines associated with a computer.

source address. Address of a storage location in Memory, or a register, containing an information item which is to be transferred to another location.

speedup. The ratio of the time to execute an efficient serial program for a calculation to the time to execute a parallel program for the same calculation on N processors identical to the serial processor.

static scheduling. A scheduling method that assigns resources to tasks in a pre-determined fashion during compile time or before.

survivability. The ability of a system to continue to function properly, despite of possibly existing conditions which may cause a failure.

synchronization. An operation in which two or more processors exchange information to coordinate their activity.

task. Synonymous to "process" by some definitions. Other definitions regard a task as a higher order structure, possibly containing a number of processes.

three-address instruction. An instruction whose format contains references to the addresses of two operands and of the destination of the operation result.

throughput. Number of processed results produced in a time unit.

two-address instruction. An instruction whose format contains references to the addresses of two operands, one of which serves both as a source and a destination.

underflow. A state in which a nonzero number becomes too small to be represented in a number system.

unlock. A primitive operation that grants processes access to a critical section.

utilization. Percentage of time a processor spends executing tasks.

virtual memory. A hierarchical storage system of at least two levels, which is managed by an Operating System to appear to a user as a single large directly addressable main memory. Synonymous to "Logical Memory."

vector arithmetic. Arithmetic operations whose operands are vectors of data.

vector computer. A computer whose instructions include instructions for vector arithmetic.

vector instruction. An instruction whose operands are vectors.

vector processor. A computing device capable of operating on vectors as basic data structures.

vector register. A register in a vector processor that holds a vector operand.

very large scale integration (VLSI). The fabrication of 100,000 or more gates on a single wafer.

Von Neumann architecture. Forms the basis of the design of a digital computer with the following properties:

1. It is composed of five basic units: ALU, Memory (M), Control, Input, Output.
2. The M is single, linear, sequentially addressed. The M is one dimensional, a vector of words, with addresses starting from 0.
3. Both the program and data are stored in the single M.
4. There is no explicit distinction between instructions and data or between various data types.

Problems

1. Explain, in detail, the difference between an MISD and an instruction pipeline.
2. Describe how is the hierarchy of levels (end of Chapter 1) implemented on the Alliant (Chapter 7).
3. Design and draw a detailed block diagram of a dual-bus, four processor, eight memory modules, and two I/O processors system. What are the basic requirements on the memory modules?
4. Develop a tree-structure interconnection of nodes for a four-cube (Figure 2.3). How many levels can one obtain? Repeat for the five-cube.
5. Design a Crosspoint Switch for an 8×8 Crossbar Network (Figures 2.4 and 2.5). Estimate the expected cost per switch and the overall cost.
6. Repeat problem 5 for 16×16 and 32×32 crossbar networks.
7. Expand the three-stage generalized cube network, shown in Figure 2.7 for eight inputs and eight outputs, into a 16 inputs and 16 outputs network. Use the same interconnection function L as in Figure 2.7. Estimate the cost ratio of the two networks mentioned above.
8. Expand the Butterfly four input–output switch, shown in Figure 2.10, into an eight input–eight output switch. Estimate the cost ratio of the two switches.
9. Repeat problem 8 for 16, 32 and 64 input-output switches.
10. Work out the example illustrated in Figure 2.11 for a three- and a four-processor model.
11. Repeat problem 10 for a case of complete overlapping between the R and C periods, assuming $R > C$.
12. Given the following FORTRAN subprogram:

$$\text{DO } 10 \text{ I} = 1,\text{N}$$
$$\text{A(I)} = \text{B(I)} + \text{C(I)}$$
$$10 \quad \text{D(I)} = \text{A(I)} * \text{E(I)}$$

$$\text{DO } 20 \text{ J} = 1,\text{N}$$
$$\text{D(I)} = \text{B(I)}/\text{F(I)}$$
$$20 \quad \text{C(I)} = \text{A(I)} - \text{G(I)}$$

$$\text{DO } 30 \text{ K} = 1,\text{N}$$
$$\text{AA(K)} = \text{BB(K)} - \text{CC(K)}$$
$$30 \quad \text{P(K)} = \text{AA(K)}/10.$$

Apply the Bernstein condition to the above three loops. Which can or can not be executed in parallel and why?

13. Use Amdahl's inequality to establish the Speedup S, for n processors, assuming that the fraction of sequentially executed instructions in the program, f = 0.1, 0.2, 0.3, 0.5, 0.75, 0.9, 0.95 (see Chapter 6). Draw graphs illustrating the change in S as a function of f using n as a parameter, with n = 2, 4, 8, 16, 32.

14. Repeat problem 13 drawing S as a function of n, using f as a parameter.

15. Applying the method of logarithmic indices (Chapter 6), the following weights were assigned:

Index	Weight
N (processors)	0.1
M (MIPS/CPU)	0.3
F (MFLOPS/CPU)	0.5
W	0
B	0
I	0
D (MBytes/sec.)	0.1

Calculate the new weighted L values for the Alliant, ELXSI, and iPSC/2.

16. Repeat problem 15. for the following weight distribution:

N	M	F	W	B	I	D
0.2	0.1	0.1	0	0	0.4	0.2

What conclusions can you draw from the results of problems 15 and 16?

17. Apply the logarithmic indices method to the Sequent and Encore systems, comparing them with the ELXSI and Alliant.

18. Repeat problem 17 for the NCUBE, FPS T-series and the Butterfly, comparing them with the iPSC /2.

Index